You Don't Need
To Read This Book
But You'll Want To...

As a Key Executive holding this book, it is obvious you are seeking ways to assure your company is top drawer by utilizing best practices, resulting in your company becoming more profitable and competitive in our new economy.

In short, this is a highly informative and systematic program for C-Suite (CEO, CFO, COO, etc.) business leaders and strategic managers who want to move quickly and accurately by leveraging the success, mistakes and wisdom of other top businesses to improve their own companies.

This is a step-by-step guide for business leaders. You will be impressed with the positive impact you'll experience on your company's status and bottom line.

What others say...

"Using a comprehensive approach, the author, an insurance professional, looks at how executives can cut their insurance costs by addressing a wide range of factors, including risk factor calculations and employee relationships. A solid overview of techniques that can help companies save money on workers' compensation and related expenses."

~Kirkus Reviews

To Chrdy
To Your Continued Success
Rick Delrupple

"The ideas revealed in **Accidents Waiting to Happen** provide user-friendly, turnkey, and proven strategies that will put you in control in the administration of a results-focused, successful workers' compensation program, whatever your industry.

"The concepts presented in this book are "spot on" for companies looking to become "Best in Class." If you truly want to become more competitive in your marketplace, it is important to understand from an insurance company perspective, employers considered "Best in Class" typically receive better pricing at renewal time."

~Eleanor Powell-Yoder, President, Michigan Commercial Insurance Mutual

"It is extremely important to pick partners who can truly help your company. In that regard, we are glad to have worked with Rick. I was amazed that in just eight short months, he dramatically lowered the number and severity of workers' compensation claims we typically had through the years, improving our profitability and lowering your operating costs. With his leadership, we effectively added over $13 million to our financial statement. I highly recommend you read his book."

~Jim Ginas, President, Southeast Modular Manufacturing

"I used to hope that I would find a way to get a better handle on the high cost of workers' compensation. After implementing the key concepts in Rick's book, I have confidence now that I can better control my operating costs helping my company to be more profitable."

~John Murphy, President, Harvest Time International

Accidents Waiting to Happen:

Best Practices in Workers' Comp Administration

and

Protecting Corporate Profitability

A Step-By-Step Guide for Business Leaders

Rick Dalrymple, CPIA, CMIP

Risk Consultant, Author, Speaker

Accidents Waiting to Happen: Best Practices in Workers' Comp
Administration and Protecting Corporate Profitability
Rick Dalrymple

© 2013 Rick Dalrymple. All rights reserved.

ISBN: 978-0-9890150-0-4
Opportunity Press
1855 West State Road 434
Longwood, FL 32750
Email: Rick.Dalrymple@ioausa.com   Web address: www.RichardDalrymple.com

This publication is designed to provide accurate and authoritative information with regard to the subject matter covered. It is sold with the understanding that the author and publisher are not engaged in rendering legal, accounting or other professional advice. If legal advice or other expert professional assistance is required, the services of a competent professional person should be sought.

For information about special discounts for bulk purchases, or speakers on this subject for your event, please contact Rick Dalrymple at 321-578-7559 or at Rick.Dalrymple@ioausa.com. All trademarks are the property of their respective companies:

Cover Design: Dan Yeager / Daniel@nu-images.com

Disclaimer: Please note that the complexities of employment law are in play with regards to workers' compensation. This book provides basic, practical information on best practices for workers' compensation administration. It is not intended as guide to the legal restrictions or procedures applicable to the employer-employee relationship or labor laws. No statement in this book should be interpreted as legal advice, nor should any organization take action relying solely on the statements contained herein. The employment relationship is highly regulated. You should consult counsel before taking any adverse employment action. The opinions and thoughts expressed in this book apply generally to all employers regardless of location and regardless of whether its relationship with its employees is governed by a collective bargaining agreement. To the extent that any insight in this book is inconsistent with any laws or union contracts, however, the information should be disregarded.

Register This Book Now!

Access additional *FREE* resources

Just go to:

__www.RichardDalrymple.com__

When you register this book, you gain immediate access to an online portal featuring a wide variety of valuable material, tools and business-building information designed to:

- Reduce Operating Costs
- Increase Profitability
- Streamline Your Company
- Avoid Employee Lawsuits
- Gain a Competitive Edge

And much more…

These materials will be updated often, as new resources become available.

I look forward to your feedback about this book, which will serve you and your company for years to come.

A portion of the profits from this book go to UCanSKi2, an organization dedicated to teaching people with disabilities to water ski, to experience the exhilaration and fulfillment of accomplishing activities that once seemed out of reach.

BE GREAT!

www.UcanSki2.com

Dedication

This book is dedicated to…

My best friend and wife of more than 31 years, Caren Dalrymple, who has been there for me and our beautiful family to steer our ship in the right direction. Your selfless, giving ways and the positive impact you have had on people give me a model to live by.

To my exceptional associate and friend, Judi Beede and to the rest of the team at IOA.

To the Ritenour family for your vision and leadership.

Together, we make a difference.

To our valued clients who have entrusted us with their trust and confidence.

And to all the new readers, associates, and friends we will meet along the way.

Accidents Waiting to Happen

TABLE OF CONTENTS

Introduction

SECTION I: Important Foundational Information

SECTION II: The Process

SECTION III: APPENDIX

Introduction

During the Great Recession, employment sagged. Workers' compensation (WC) costs fell, as fewer people were employed and they filed fewer claims.

That's no surprise, as history shows: workers' comp claims fall during a recession, and then rise sharply, as employment increases. Sooner or later, every company faces a workers' compensation claim. If the claim turns into a lawsuit, costs can rise exponentially. In many cases, these incidents are completely avoidable.

Most companies today are far more vulnerable than their executives imagine. Often, the greatest threat comes from inside the company. These risks can be traced back to inadequate hiring practices and inattention to operational policies and procedures.

Even when company's written policies and procedures mirror best practices for workers' comp, without the full support of company execs and communication across the organization, they won't be fully implemented. If these policies and procedures are not part of every employee's daily performance, the company is headed for trouble.

In fact, when companies get complacent about hiring, supervision, and training-- they are creating accidents waiting to happen, leaving the company wide open to claims and lawsuits.

WC claims not only pose a risk to short-term profits, they threaten morale, reduce productivity, and impair workplace safety, among other hazards. Where do you stand?

Question: How confident are you about your company's workplace policies and procedures, and your ability to stay current and compliant with state and federal employment laws?

- ❒ Absolutely certain

- ❒ Somewhat certain

- ❒ Uncertain

- ❒ Don't know

Whatever answer you choose, if you don't know your company's *RiskScore®*, you're just guessing-- or maybe hoping-- things will be all right. If that's good enough for you, good luck.

If hiding your head in the sand isn't for you, read on...

To avert almost certain hikes in WC costs, the C-Suite (CEO, CFO, COO, etc.) has to be involved in the solution.

Don't take my word for it.

In one of the most influential business books of the past 15 years, *Execution,* Larry Bossity and Ram Charon point out a misunderstanding all too common among business executives. Leaders confuse execution-- actually getting things done-- with tactics. Execution is not just tactics-- it's a discipline and a system. It has to be built into a company's strategy, its goals, and its culture. And the leader of the organization must be deeply engaged in it.

So then, is that light or a train at the end of your tunnel?

If you've ever dealt with the frustration, lost productivity, and the direct/indirect costs of employee WC claims and lawsuits, you might want to pay attention.

For a variety of factors, WC claims surge following a recession. Why? New jobs tend to pay less, workers often receive less training, and there will be more claims as the number of job opportunities increase.

Some employers imagine they're protected by the WC policies they pay for. In fact, the way the system works, your premium costs and the amounts paid on WC claims can make a serious dent in your net profits, especially as claims increase in both number and severity.

Insurance alone won't protect your bottom line.

To avoid opening up your company to significant increased costs, it's time to pay attention, once again, to operations-- and to best practices surrounding hiring, training, and claims management.

Start with an organization-wide risk assessment. It can be made easy, it's worthwhile, and could save you a bundle of money while significantly reducing your risk. It takes focus and it takes implementing a system of strategic business practices. That's where you come in.

You don't need to do it all yourself, but you must be involved. Most companies can reach the standard of "best practices." Once you understand what's at stake, you can take systematic steps to improve your operations across the organization.

You'll then want to communicate your intense commitment to achieving your goals-- and acknowledge the importance of an engaged workforce. Once you know the game plan, you can get everyone on the same page; even attract WC champions among your employees. Win in this arena and you not only avoid escalating WC costs, you also stand to win in the competition for the best employees.

Here's one thing that may surprise you. Going through the process I describe in this book will enable you not only to reduce your risk; you'll also save money directly and indirectly. It's time to focus on sustainability for the long haul.

1. Increase your profitability

2. Reduce your operating costs

3. Avoid business risk that you may be totally unaware of

4. Improve your competitiveness in the global marketplace.

As you embark on your journey to better profitability, I hope you discover that this book gives you a fantastic start, by providing a trustworthy map to direct you on your way.

IMAGINE... better hiring procedures that reduce your number of claims by over 60% and the severity of those claims by over 21%.

IMAGINE... access to compliance ready, profit-enhancing procedures that save you time and money.

IMAGINE... procedures to avoid employee lawsuits.

IMAGINE.... well-organized claim activity, enabling you to close claims faster and for less money, preventing lost corporate profits.

IMAGINE... access to streamlined and lower-cost training and easily identified trend reports.

IMAGINE... the ability to quickly determine your company's strengths and pinpoint areas for improvement, and achieving "Best Practices" status in workers' comp administration, saving your company hundreds of thousands of dollars in lost profits.

Why not get started now?

Navigational information about this book:

Accidents Waiting to Happen contains 3 sections:

Section 1: (pages 17-80) Provides insights and case studies that explain "why" the deployment of specific policies and procedures are critical to your company's profitability.

Section 2: (pages 82-188) Is the heart of the book which provides the solutions and strategies considered Best Practices in workers' comp administration.

Section 3: (pages 189-247) Provides the Appendix which contains further details and explanations to the strategies shared in section 2.

"We are what we repeatedly do; excellence, then, is not an act but a habit."

~Aristotle

SECTION I

Important Foundational Material

If you are serious about driving positive results to your company's bottom line, understand "WHY" you should do certain things.

Once you understand the impact of risk on your company's bottom line, it will make more sense when deploying the process shared with you in Section II.

Chapter 1:

Four Keys for Competitiveness in the New Economy

Any successful business person today knows you have to drive positive results to be competitive in your marketplace. You do have to continually look for ways to cut costs, improve staff efficiency, and drive sales.

In the past couple of years, many companies have seen their profit margins squeezed by forces outside their control. I spoke with a manufacturing company executive accustomed to a 30% net-profit before the "Great Recession" hit in 2008. Today, he hopes for a 10% net-profit margin, and hates the fact that he may never see his customary profit margins again.

Some of you would be happy to receive a 10% net-profit margin, because your business is hanging by a thread, glad for a 1 to 3% net-profit margin. Unfortunately, many businesses have closed their doors in the past few years.

Some of you need money to purchase new capital equipment or repair your current equipment to stay competitive. If you can relate to any of these issues, read on. This book is filled with insights and strategies designed to help you do the following:

1. Increase your profitability
2. Lower your operating costs
3. Reduce business risks you may be unaware of
4. Make you more competitive in your marketplace

I will show you how to lower the human and financial costs of your workers' compensation program. Specifically, I will review the policies and procedures you should have in place to accomplish the goals listed above. I will also share with you some tools used by companies today to streamline big-ticket areas, including training and claims management.

To be competitive long-term in this new economy, you have to be profitable. Profitable businesses today have put good habits in place that are considered "best practices." They have created a great culture within their organizations that supports the overall initiatives of senior management.

Who should read this book?

This book is designed for CEOs, CFOs, COOs, Risk Managers, HR Directors, Administrators, Safety Directors and Claim Coordinators. I offer a comprehensive "holistic approach" to an integrated system to all levels of company management. Some material will speak the language C-Suite executives relate to. But there will also be material that needs to be carried out by others within the organization, and communicated to by everyone within your company.

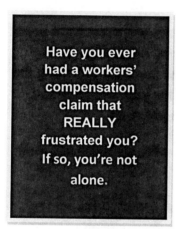

Have you ever had a workers' compensation claim that REALLY frustrated you? If so, you're not alone.

C-Suite executives need to understand the impact of a poorly managed worker's compensation system on their bottom line. They can then lead their management team to begin setting goals and deploying the strategies and tactics found in this book.

Have you ever had a workers' compensation claim that REALLY frustrated you? If so, you're not alone. What frustrated you most? Was it the carrier? The employee? Did you feel like you were paddling alone in the proverbial canoe headed straight for the waterfall?

This book is not about theory. Instead, it contains practical insights and easy-to-follow instructions to help you navigate the complex topic of effective workers' compensation administration for greater profitability. Have you ever looked for a resource to give you a greater sense of control when dealing with workers' compensation? Now you have one!

Here is what I would like you to achieve with this book.

My sincere desire is that you acquire a clear understanding of how to administer a successful workers' compensation program in your business. I've broken the program into easy-to-manage steps, which are all part of a system called the "PX4" process.

Here is the good news.

The "PX4" process works! Your company will experience fewer claims and those claims will cost you less, on average. It may take time to deploy the steps mapped out here; but following the "PX4"process, will drive better results for your company and make you more competitive in your marketplace.

Let's look at an example of a manufacturing company and their workers' comp results.

The Table 1.1 below shows what happened when the manufacturing company began using the "PX4" process.

Table 1.1 Coverage: Workers Compensation				
Policy Term	# Claims	Total Incurred	Earned Premium	Loss Ratio
2012-2013	29	$27,381.23	$262,622.56	10.43%
2011-2012	46	$182,170.96	$179,763.39	101.34%
2010-2011	36	$519,860.56	$173,010.58	300.48%
2009-2010	27	$254,347.51	$212,554.00	119.66%
TOTAL	138	$983,760.26	$827,950.53	132.98%

From 2009 to 2011, this company averaged 36 workers'
compensation claims per year, and $318,793 in "total incurred
losses." The term "total incurred losses" refers to the combination
of the amount actually paid by the insurance company in claims,
plus any reserves that are projected by the carrier to be paid
during the remainder of the claim. As you can see in Table 1.2
below, in 2012, their losses plummeted 91%, from more than
$182,000 to under $28,000.

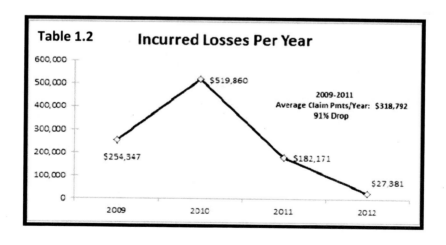

See Table 1.3 below. The manufacturer's "loss ratio," (claims divided by premiums) averaged 173.82% from 2009 to 2011. To put this into perspective, insurance underwriters prefer to see loss ratios below 40%.

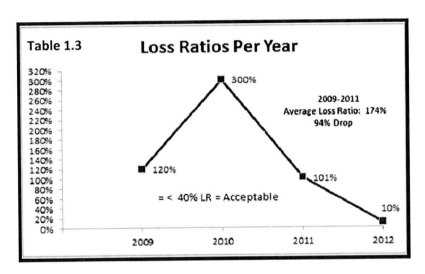

Referring back to Table 1.2, look at the difference between 2012 losses compared to their three-year-average losses ($318,793 − $27,381 = $291,412). In other words, the company had a direct loss savings of $291,412. I will talk more about indirect loss costs and the impact on sales in a later chapter, but based upon their loss savings, they effectively added over $13 million in sales to their company's top line.

Said another way, if the company's workers' comp claims caused $291,000 in losses, when you include all total loss costs (including indirect costs), they would have had to generate over $13 million in additional dollars in sales to maintain the same profit margin.

Let me ask you another question.

Are these the kind of results you want for your company?

If you answered yes, you are on your way to building a profitable and more competitive company.

Importance of goals

I hope you discover the importance of goal setting on improving your workers' compensation "system". While all of you have workers' comp policies, do you know what your goals are for your workers' comp "system?" After reading this book, I suspect many of you will increase your expectations for your workers' comp program performance. This book will help you formulate specific goals for managing a workers' comp process that will help improve your profitability.

When I refer to "workers compensation", (WC) it is not about having a competitive workers' comp "policy", but about having a holistic workers' comp "system" in place designed to produce better results for your entire company – results that far exceed the cost of the workers' comp policy itself.

Here's what I mean.

You can have purchased the best WC product on the market, but if you don't have an effective "system" in place, you can easily lose money. Having a good WC policy without a "system" is like buying the most energy-efficient air-conditioning unit, and leaving the windows open on a hot summer day. The point is, with no "system" in place, the actual workers' compensation policy you buy should be a secondary decision.

Here's one good reason to make time to master this material: you want to remain competitive.

Do you want your competitors to pass you by?

Your competitors may already be implementing the strategies outlined in upcoming chapters.

If you want a competitive edge, read on.

"Insanity: doing the same thing over and over again and expecting different results."

~ *Albert Einstein*

Chapter 2:

Reduce Business Risk = Increase Profitability

When people think of higher profits, they usually think about a rise in sales. In this chapter, I illustrate at how business risk leads to business losses, which reduces your profitability as a company. Said another way, if you reduce your company's business risk, you can increase your profitability.

In his book, *"Consultative Brokerage: A Value Strategy* "Rob Ekern outlines four types of risk most companies face:

1. Strategic Risk - created by customer, products, and competitors.

2. Operational Risk – from supply chain/business interruption risks, brand/reputation risks, human resources, IT systems and audit.

3. Hazard Risks – losses from property, liability, workers' compensation/ safety issues, and legal/environmental.

4. Financial Risks – generated by asset price volatility, interest rates, commodities or the weather.

This book, " Accidents Waiting to Happen: Best Practices in Workers' Comp Administration and Protecting Corporate Profitability" is designed to help you make sure you have proper operating policies and procedures in place; which in turn, will help reduce the level of strategic, operational, financial, and hazard risks facing your company. Bottom line, when you reduce your business risk, you will in turn, increase your profitability as a company.

Why should this concern you?

Did you know that the average settlement costs of lawsuits that do not even go to trial, settle for over $32,000. For those cases that actually go to trial, the average settlement costs are in excess of $310,000.

Average cost of case $32,000 (Non-trial)

Average cost of case $310,000 (Trial)

Let's say an employee who decides to take you to task over a legal issue, is asking for a relatively small amount, $15,000. How much do you think that lawsuit will cost your company?

After you consider all the dynamics: lost productivity and your valuable time to deal with the issue, experts say that small $15,000 claim would have cost you in excess of $50,000. Let's further say that your company currently maintains a 4% net-profit margin. How much sales do you have to generate to make up for that $15,000 claim? In this example, the answer is over $1,250,000. ($50,000/.04 = $1,250,000). Surprised?

How much risk does your company face?

As a leader in your organization, I trust you are continually looking for ways to run more efficiently as a company. You may have taken the time to identify and evaluate the biggest perceived threats to your company by going through a "risk survey" to identify your potential threats.

Find out your *RiskScore*®

If you have gone through a "risk survey" in the last couple of years, good job. If not, consider putting it on your "TO DO" list. One of the quickest and easiest ways to conduct a risk survey is to find out your *RiskScore*®.

Your *RiskScore*® helps you determine your strengths and weaknesses as a company as they relate to your business risk. Once you know your risk factors, you are in a better position to address them.

Most business leaders consider hazard risk, as their biggest threat to shareholder value. Actually, this is least likely to affect your bottom line, versus the other types of risks.

Why?

The answer is: because hazard risks are largely addressed when buying insurance policies, which enable you to transfer your risk to an insurance carrier.

The biggest threats to your company come from "strategic" and "operational risks." How effectively you run your company operationally, will impact your ability to be profitable and strategic in your marketplace. See the chapter four - "Total Cost of Risk," for more detail.

2.1 **When Companies Lose Value**
Which Risk is Greatest?

(The National Underwriter Co.)

In this book, I will look more closely at how caustic claims can be to your company's profitability. I will also suggest steps you can take to protect your company from claims.

"Too many leaders fool themselves into thinking their companies are well run."

~Larry Bossity & Ram Charon, Execution

Chapter 3:

Workers' Compensation Frustrations?

Let me start off by re-asking you this question:

Have you ever had a REALLY frustrating workers' compensation claim or have you heard of any of your business friends complain about one?

If you are like many executives, your answer is a resounding "YES." I suspect you are keenly aware of two points:

1. Not all insurance companies are created equal. Most carriers do an honorable job managing claims; however, insurance companies have goals and initiatives in the settlement of claims that may not match your goals and initiatives as an employer.
2. Insurance claims cost you money. Big money. And, depending upon how they are managed, can determine your profitability as a company.

Most insurance companies do an honorable job in the management of claims, but may have left you feeling frustrated during the claims process by a lack of communication. This is an important issue.

Effective communication?

Lack of communication is not necessarily intentional, but it is a symptom of a much bigger problem. Many insurance claims adjusters are overwhelmed with caseloads that are difficult to manage. Insurance companies have been affected by the economy just like you have. They have had to do more with fewer employees, just like you. In years past, the average caseload per adjuster per month ranged from 100 to 250 claim files. Today, it has been reported that some adjusters have caseloads as high as 250 to 300 claim files per month.

If that is the case, this begs the question; do you really think the adjuster has time to manage your claims they have on their desk?

You can answer that question without help. The reality is, the adjuster is working diligently to process a mountain of paperwork but does not have time to proactively manage cases that could result in better outcomes.

Later in this book, I will share with you simple steps to help the adjuster immensely, which will improve your claim results.

The financial impact

While adjusters have a difficult job, and should be commended for their abilities to manage the claims process, in reality, adjusters many times do not understand the financial impact that claims have on your company.

Start with your Experience Modification Factor

What is an experience modification (mod) factor? An experience mod is a factor assigned to your company by the National Council on Compensation Insurance (NCCI) based on your prior loss history.

One thing to keep in mind is that your experience modification factor could be higher than necessary for a couple of reasons.

1. It could be higher because your claim cases are not being managed effectively.

2. It could be higher because NCCI (National Council on Compensation Insurance) made clerical mistakes during the experience modification calculation process.

To address item 1, make sure your claim cases are closed as quickly as possible. I have seen cases where high reserves set on files were not reduced when they could have been. Lowering your case reserves, when warranted, has the effect of lowering your experience mod factor, which ultimately reduces your premium.

Rating worksheet review

To address item 2 above, have your NCCI Experience Modification Rating Worksheet reviewed for accuracy. I have seen cases where insurance companies have reduced a claim reserve, but NCCI never updated their filings to reflect those changes. Consequently, when NCCI calculated the mod for a given company, they used higher claim amounts leading to higher-than-necessary mod factors.

I have also seen NCCI accidentally calculate an experience modification factor inaccurately, by using lower payroll amounts, which has the effect of increasing your mod factor. That's why I said, you should have a professional review your experience modification for accuracy. Put this on your "TO DO" list if you have not done so in the last 12 months.

Have you ever been curious to know your company's lowest possible experience modification factor?

There is a simple way to calculate this number. You need the latest copy of your NCCI experience modification rating worksheet. Divide your actual "stabilized" claim values by your expected claim totals shown in a box with the letter "K" in the upper left-hand corner. For a brief two-minute video that explains this process, go to http://tiny.cc/eoh0uw.

Look at the Appendix page 234 to better understand the impact that an "experience modification" can have on your profitability.

Success rests on your shoulders

One of my goals is that you learn to play an important role in claims processing, enabling your adjuster to help you reduce the cost of your claims. My team's philosophy is 70% of your success in the proper management of your workers' comp program rests on your shoulders as the employer, not the insurance company's.

Moving ahead

I will share best practices you can deploy to keep you and your adjuster on the same page in the processing of your claim. You'll get better results – and lower your operational costs.

"Our greatest glory is not in never failing,
but in rising every time we fall."

~Confucius

Chapter 4:

Total Cost of Risk

In order to understand the financial impact of losses on your company, it is time for you to embrace the concept of "Total Cost of Risk."

Total Cost of Risk (also known as TCOR) is not theory, but a practical viewpoint of how risk impacts your bottom line. The study of TCOR has been around for many years. Back in 1974, Frank E. Bird Jr. began researching this topic. He was known for his publication entitled "The Real Cost of Accidents Can Be Measured and Controlled."

Let me ask you a few questions

Have you ever had an employee who left your company after just five, six or seven months of work? Did they leave because of a workers' comp injury? Did you let them go because of poor performance, or did they leave for a better job opportunity?

How much did your last bad hire cost you?

Poor hires cost you more than you may imagine. Take this example. An employee earning $35,000 leaves your company after six months. How much do you think that employee cost your company? Conservatively speaking, the cost is in excess of $70,000 when you take into account all the indirect hidden costs of losing an employee. Really stop and think; how much did your last bad hire cost you?

Now consider this. If you were to add all your insurance premium costs, what would your total be? Go ahead, take a few seconds, total up all your insurance premium costs, and jot that number down. Include not only your workers' compensation coverage, but also your property, liability, automobile, and health insurance costs, etc.

Do you have that number written down? Fix it in your mind; we will come back to that in just a moment.

The indirect hidden costs of losing an employee can be found with issues like:

1. The cost to rehire a new employee
2. The cost to retrain a new employee
3. Lost productivity
4. Lower morale of existing employees
5. Management time in dealing with the issue

Now, return to the question. How much do you pay in insurance premiums each year? For example, if your insurance premiums totaled $100,000, the study of TCOR would suggest that your "Total Cost of Risk" could be in excess of $1 million.

The easiest way to remember this is to picture an iceberg. What you pay in insurance premiums only represents the tip of the iceberg. What is below the waterline, which represents your indirect business costs, is where you should concentrate your management efforts.

Look at table 4.1 below.

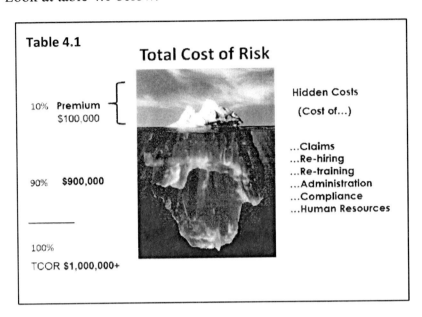

Table 4.1

Total Cost of Risk

10% Premium $100,000

90% $900,000

100%

TCOR $1,000,000+

Hidden Costs

(Cost of...)

...Claims
...Re-hiring
...Re-training
...Administration
...Compliance
...Human Resources

Think about this. When insurance agents or brokers come to talk to you about your insurance program, where is the typical emphasis of the conversation? It typically is about your policies, premiums and coverage. Right?

The lion's share of your costs

This begs the question, if the lion's share of your costs come from issues that are below the waterline in the iceberg example we just talked about, wouldn't it make more sense to immediately and effectively address those issues?

It is always important to find ways to reduce your direct costs, secure better coverage when possible, and seek out better "proactive" service if you feel the relationship with your agent has changed from when you first started working with them.

Assume that your interaction with an agent netted you a 10% savings on your $100,000 premium after having gone through a quoting exercise. You just saved $10,000, which in anyone's book is good money. So, what was discussed or done to reduce your indirect costs? If a consultant was to save you that same 10% on your entire "Total Cost of Risk," that represents a savings of approximately $100,000.

I don't know about you, but when given the option, most smart businesses want to look at TCOR in a holistic manner. They understand the importance of having good coverage, but they understand it is more important to address those issues below the waterline that you can't see easily.

Insurance buying decisions based on premiums

Let me give you an example of the consequences of making insurance buying decisions based on premiums. This cost a company more than $76,000 in unnecessary insurance premiums.

A manufacturer was in the process of evaluating two insurance proposals for their January 1 renewal. In one hand, he had his renewal from his current insurance agent whose premium total was $102,000. The coverage seemed to be complete, and to the best of "his" knowledge, he was receiving sound operational advice. In the other hand, he had a risk management proposal from a firm whose premium total was $113,000. The two proposals and subsequent coverage summaries seemed "apples to apples;" however, sound risk management was not a priority in their decision-making process. A Risk Assessment did not seem important at the time. Ultimately, they paid a high price.

Here is what happened.

The employer decided to stay with its current agent for several reasons. The premium was lower, they were comfortable with the current relationship, and service levels seemed to meet their expectations from what "they knew." Recall the saying, "Sometimes you don't know what you don't know"? Well, that is what happened in this case and it cost this employer a lot of money.

The employer paid its renewal deposit to their carrier and received their needed Certificates of Insurance. Little did they know that some of their business practices were setting them up for a costly mistake, one that could have been avoided.

Four months after renewal, the manufacturer ended up with a claim that cost $76,000 in additional premium, due to a failure to administer some simple procedures (medical health questionnaire, background verification, integrity testing) in the hiring process (more on this later). Instead of paying $102,000 in premiums, their ultimate insurance costs were $178,000 (versus $113,000) for that year.

Reducing your risk

I know you are extremely busy, and that most employers prefer to "deal" with insurance on an annual basis; however, the purchase of policies is only a part of the process. Looking at your business practices and reducing your risk is critically important to your profitability. That's why risk management is something that is addressed by "best practices" companies throughout the year, not just at your policy renewal. The trick is finding relationships able to provide turnkey solutions that drive results to your bottom line, freeing up your time to do what you do best.

Now I ask you, is it better to make buying decisions for your insurance program based upon the cost of premiums, or from a holistic viewpoint in which you review risk management issues?

A Risk Assessment is something to consider implementing on an annual basis.

Bottom line, it is important to seek out relationships with firms who can provide your organization resources designed to lower your "Total Cost of Risk (TCOR)." Throughout this book, I will help you understand the types of resources to look for, which many companies are using successfully today to lower their TCOR and improve their competitive advantage.

*"Only those who dare to fail greatly
can ever achieve greatly."*

~John F. Kennedy

Chapter 5:

Indirect Loss Cost Factors

To better understand the science of TCOR (Total Cost of Risk), let's look at what are called "Indirect Loss Cost Factors." Indirect losses are a real, but often hidden losses your business may be sustaining.

OSHA (Occupational Safety and Health Administration) has given us a hand in that regard. OSHA publishes statistics for different types of claims companies sustain: workers' compensation, general liability, automobile, property, etc. These add real additional costs to any claim your company incurs, even if difficult to measure.

Indirect loss cost

To determine those additional costs of your claims, according to OSHA, you should multiply an indirect loss cost factor to each of your claims. It is not an exact science because there are so many variables involved in calculating indirect costs, but suffice to say, indirect loss costs exist.

In *Consultative Brokerage: A Value Strategy*, Rob Ekern illustrates the indirect loss cost factors to apply to your claims in order to determine the true total cost of your claim.

Take a look at Table 5.1, which illustrate indirect loss cost factors (ILCF) for workers' compensation coverage. You will notice that the ILCFs are different depending on claim size. For those claims under $3000, OSHA suggests a multiple of 4.5. As the claim values increase, the ILCF decrease.

Department of Labor

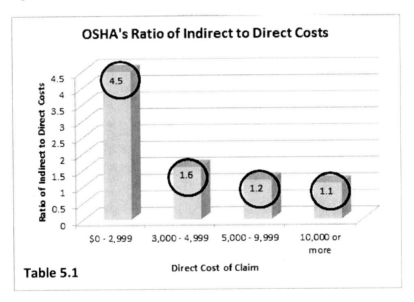

Table 5.1

As Table 5.1 shows, a workers' compensation claim of $10,000, multiplied by a factor of 1.1, as OSHA recommends, the total cost of that claim would be $21,000. As another example, a workers' compensation claim totaling $2000 could cost your company over $9000 ($2,000 x 4.5).

Most experts consider these OSHA ratios to be conservative, especially in the area of workers' comp, because they do not take into account the impact caused by the increase to your experience modification factor.

Take the time

Schedule time soon to take your claims loss runs and multiply your respective types of claims by the indirect loss cost factors shown above, to see just how much your claims really cost your company. Although our focus has been on workers' comp, you can see that indirect loss costs impact many facets of your company.

If you are successful at controlling your workers' compensation claims, you will typically find an improvement in other areas of your business. My plan is to help you accomplish this goal, so read on.

Had you ever wanted to use a quick tool that can help you in determining your additional costs of claims? OSHA's website has a great tool that enables you to calculate the annual costs of your accidents, as well as their impact on your profits and sales. Go to http://tiny.cc/06bcow for a tool that enables you to calculate your costs based on your company's specific factors.

Dramatic impact your bottom line

Even though it can be difficult to quantify indirect loss costs, they are very real and they dramatically impact your bottom line. In the next chapter, I will take you through a case study of a company where management took the time to actually calculate their additional costs of loss. Buy-in from senior management means they understand how indirect loss costs impact the company. Then it gets much easier to communicate this message to your staff and validate the importance of Risk Management. Once your staff changes their behavior to support a safe working environment, you will be on the road to higher profitability.

"Every morning you are handed 24 golden hours. They are one of the few things in this world that you get free of charge. If you had all the money in the world, you couldn't buy an extra hour. What will you do with this priceless treasure?"

~Anonymous

Chapter 6:

Case Study

Up to this point, we have discussed Total Cost of Risk and Indirect Loss Cost Factors, and their key role in assessing your risk vulnerability.

Now, let me share a case study with you.

The illustration 6.1 below shows the cost of eight automobile and workers' comp claims a client sustained in one year. In this case, company losses totaled $87,253, and the client paid $12,000 in deductibles, while the insurance company paid $75,253.

Table 6.1	Case Study	
Company losses on 8 claims		$87,253
Company deductibles paid		$12,000
Insurance company paid		$75,253

See illustration 6.2 below. When this company took the time to review the impact of losses on their company, they determined they had lost $93,550.

Client summary of direct / indirect costs		
Client paid deductibles	$12,000	Direct
Experience Modification increase (3 years)	$18,481	Indirect
Increase in insurance premiums	$13,716	Indirect
Clean up costs	$ 2,310	Indirect
Loss of production	$14,108	Indirect
Repair & replaced asset (depreciation)	$12,883	Indirect
Legal	$ 2,400	Indirect
Training employees	$ 6,852	Indirect
Administrative time (paperwork)	$ 2,400	Indirect
Staff & supervisor time	$ 6,800	Indirect
Your time (8 hours @ $200 per hour)	$ 1,600	Indirect
Table 6.2	**Total $93,550**	

Surprised?

How did they arrive at this number?

Take a moment to scan the list of items. Clearly, the cost of their deductible was a direct and easy cost to measure. Obviously, without the claims, they wouldn't have needed to pay deductibles. But the indirect costs on the list were a bit more challenging to calculate.

Additional costs

With the help of a sophisticated forecasting model, we determined these claims were likely to impact their experience modification factors over the next three years, which cost them an additional $18,481 in premiums.

The losses they sustained caused them to lose premium discounts they had received the previous year on their corporate automobile policy. Their reduction in premium discounts cost them an additional $13,716 at their next renewal.

Two employees who sustained work comp injuries were out of work for more than six weeks. One of those employees left the company. Based upon their hourly pay, senior management projected lost productivity costs of over $14,108. To make matters worse, the company now needed to hire and train a new employee, which would require additional time and resources.

No doubt about it: your time is valuable. Not only did the company lose productivity, employee morale dipped during this period because they were expected to pick up the slack.

Fortunately, these claims did not generate a large need for legal intervention. Given the complexities of the issues involved, they needed direction from their attorney, which cost them $2,400.

The illustration below (6.3) shows the real cost of these eight claims. When you add the $87,253 in paid losses to the $93,550 in additional loss costs, Total Loss Costs came to $180,803. ($87,243 + $93,550)

Table 6.3	**Case Study**
	$87,253 in Losses
	+
	$93,550 in Additional Costs
	$180,803 Total Loss Costs

Even more interesting than the details on indirect costs, were the observations from management. After having gone through this process, they realized their losses:

- "really shouldn't have occurred."
- "with a little bit of training, our losses could have been avoided."
- "had we had certain operational procedures in place from a claims management standpoint, our claim costs would have been lower."

Review company operations

This case study emphasizes the fact that claims cost your business significant profits. Put on your "TO DO" list, time to have a review of your company operations, specifically in the areas of Hiring, Training and Claims Management. I will expand on this topic in an upcoming chapter.

"I feel that luck is preparation meeting opportunity."

~Oprah Winfrey

Chapter 7:

Impact on Sales

I've talked about the impact of claims on your bottom line. Now, I'll talk about the impact of claims on your top line -- on your company revenue.

This is a simple calculation and a revelation for many businesses. Most people have never learned about the impact of claims on company sales.

To do this calculation, start with your company's net-profit margin.

See illustration 7.1 below. Recall the example from the preceding chapter, in which a company sustained $87,253 in paid losses, and an additional $93,550 in loss costs for a total of $180,803. This client's net-profit margin was 5%.

Table 7.1   **Sales Impact**

Net Profit Margin   **5 %**

Loss Costs $180,803 / .05 = $3,616,060

Extra Sales Needed to Pay for Those Losses

Controlling claims

If you divide 5% into $180,803 ($180,803/.05) you would get $3,616,060. The $3,616,060 represents the extra sales necessary to offset the losses they sustained.

Look at this from another perspective. By controlling claims, this company has effectively added $3,616,060 in sales. Every dollar in profit you retain eliminates the need to generate significantly more sales dollars to maintain your financial position.

As I shared previously, this management team realized, to their deep frustration, that simple safety training could have prevented those losses.

Imagine what $180,803 in lost profits would mean to your company. For many companies, that's a difficult loss to sustain.

Inventory your business

Here's another item for your "TO DO" list. Take inventory of your current business. Do you need additional capital equipment to run more efficiently or to become more competitive in your marketplace? Are you looking to expand your fleet of vehicles? Whatever your financial needs are right now, controlling claims can move you closer to your goals faster than improving on sales alone.

*"We are made to persist. That is how
we find out who we are."*

~Tobias Wolff

Chapter 8:

Everyone Needs TLC

In order to reduce your company's business risk and promote higher profitability, take a three-pronged approach to your risk management program.

Getting serious about controlling claims begins by providing your company with what we affectionately call "TLC." Yes, everyone needs a little love, and successful organizations are proactive in deploying TLC, which stands for:

On the surface, this may sound basic. But by mapping out a system for these three important areas, you can dramatically impact your company's profitability, as you saw above.

Training / Loss Prevention / Safety Programs

Training is important, but let's face it; many times training becomes a back burner issue. I understand when times are tough, it is important to make sales, but not at the expense of having losses.

Financial impact of claims

You now understand the financial impact that claims can have upon your company. The trick now is trying to find the most cost effective way to facilitate training within your company.

The Carrot or the Stick

First, let's talk about your safety culture and the most effective methods for reducing losses due to claims. Which do you think is more effective, the "Carrot" or a "Stick" management style?

Do you think that providing people positive reinforcement (the carrot) for being safe is more effective? Or do you think that providing negative reinforcement (the stick) is the best way to affect positive safety results?

Now this may surprise you. Neither strategy has statistically been proven successful in and of itself. Studies provide limited support for both approaches.

What has proven to be most successful today? The answer lies in being able to effectively administer a sound "Behavior Based Safety" (BBS) system, which incorporates both carrot and stick management.

Getting and Keeping Employee Buy-in for your Safety System

An effective BBS system identifies key behaviors that create risks and losses, and includes a process to measure behavioral activities for future review and realignment.

For a BBS system to work, two things need to happen:

- Senior leadership must fully embrace it, and,

- The system must be communicated throughout the organization.

Bottoms up?

Most BBS systems start out as a top-down system. When implemented and communicated effectively, your BBS system will flip to become a bottom-to-top system. When employees understand and buy-in to the system, they become the main engine for its continued success, not upper management.

Take an honest look at how safety is administered within your company. While most companies have the intention to deploy a successful safety program, too often, that isn't the outcome. Many companies rely on the loss control activities from their insurance carrier, but this approach is ineffective in lowering claims.

Like the rest of us, insurance companies have to do more with less staff. Their loss control personnel have had to cover more territory than in the past. Did you ever receive what sounded like generic feedback from your carrier loss control representative – suggestions that had little impact on controlling claims in your specific situation?

Measure the behaviors that need to be addressed

I have worked with a number of carriers through the years, and employers often tell me those visits were not productive. Not all carriers are created equal. Some carrier loss control representatives do a better job than others. Most carriers work hard to be relevant and helpful to the policyholders they serve. It's important that you receive tools and support that can drive better results.

Let's face it, you can have the most thorough, comprehensive safety manual in the world designed specifically for your company, but that manual alone will not drive positive results. As I said before, successful results are driven by implementing an effective system to measure the behaviors that need to be addressed.

Where do you start?

First, you'll need copies of your company's loss reports going back at least five years, so you can see the claim trends.

How easy is it to map your own claims data? I warn you, don't be surprised if your request for these reports produces a flood of information, all very difficult to interpret.

This is one good reason to work with organizations that can map out your claim trends for you, quickly and easily. At a minimum, request that your loss information include the following:

1. Losses by a body part (Arm, Head, Shoulder, Knee etc.)
2. Losses by type of Injury (Contusion, Strain, Laceration, fracture, etc.)
3. Losses by time of day and day of week

4. Losses by tenure of employee
5. Losses by job title

I'll discuss this more later in the section on Claims Management Systems.

The bottom line is to invest money in safety areas where you have specific needs. Those will become evident from your claims loss reports. More information on BBS systems is provided in the appendix of this book page number 191.

Learning Management Systems (LMS):

Systems that make training easy to deploy are becoming widespread within companies today. These Learning Management Systems (LMS) offer an easy approach to deliver and keep track of all the training done in your company, whether web-based or live training (on or off-site).

Most companies have a combination of live training programs, which can be supplemented by having access to other training that can be taught via the web.

If you are looking for a Learning Management System, here is what you should be looking for.

1. **Ease-Of-Use**. If it is not easy to use, it won't be used.

2. **Holistic library of material**. You'll find some very good LMSs on the market that are OSHA specific. Other systems may concentrate within certain disciplines. Look for LMSs that provide access to a wide variety of topics including HR compliance, Safety Training, OSHA compliance, and Wellness Training.

3. **Create Groups**. Within your company, you may have various locations, in addition to multiple departments. For ease-of-use, your LMS should give you the ability to create groups. As an example, if your company had different types of personnel, from clerical staff to maintenance workers or field workers, being able to set specific training for each group is a timesaver. The next time you hire a new field employee, simply add this employee to the right group in your LMS. They'll be automatically connected to the training for that group to take, saving you a lot of time creating individual programs for employees, one at a time.

4. **Tracking**. Since most companies need a combination of live and web-based training, make sure your LMS has the ability to track all training that is done within your company. If OSHA ever knocks on your door and wants you to produce your training records on a certain topic, with a few clicks, you can produce reports immediately.

5. **Intranet Storage**. Most training involves resource material you want employees to access. Whether you provide training to a single department or to multiple locations, a good LMS has the capacity to store the policies and procedures you want accessible to your staff, thus providing consistency throughout your organization.

6. **Reporting**. Any good LMS makes it easy to create detailed and customized reports for senior management or for outside organizations like OSHA.

7. **Create your own programs**. Some learning management systems enable you to create your own proprietary material, which can be a great timesaver in the "On-

Boarding" process. For example, some companies create their own employee orientation message. This has been a particularly useful feature for multi-location companies that want to deliver a consistent message to all new employees.

In researching online training platforms, you will find that most charge $20-$35 per employee per class. Some classes are more expensive. Some insurance carriers will provide industry-specific classes for your employees at discount rates, possibly in the range of $10 per employee per class. Check with your carrier for details.

Claims Management Systems:

Claims Management is a critical component of profitability in administering your workers' comp program.

Just as successful companies have begun using Learning Management Systems, they are also adopting automated claims management (CM) systems, which save a lot of time managing existing claims.

A CM system helps management stay on top of active claims, and automatically provides the analytics and claim trends needed to answer the "root cause analysis" questions I will discuss later.

If you are looking to streamline and organize your claim files, and you want access to a CM system, look for these features:

1. **Single entry platform**: Currently, most people submit claims to their workers' comp carrier via a phone call or fax. In preparing any claim, the same information you need to provide the carrier can be easily entered on your computer, and with the click of a button, you can email

your claim report directly to your insurance company. Protocols can be put in place so that you get validation from the carrier of their receipt of your claim.

2. **OSHA Logs**: Do you like completing OSHA logs? Few people do. With CM systems, the information you input can be used to automatically update your OSHA logs at the same time. This will save you a lot of frustration if an OSHA representative ever knocks on your door and wants to see your OSHA logs. With the click of a few buttons, your OSHA report will be available to you. Have you ever questioned which claims need to be filed on your OSHA logs and which ones do not? If you are unsure about how to determine which claims are considered recordable events or just want a little more information, go to http://tiny.cc/mtyepw for a free Excel worksheet that will walk you through a series of questions so you can tell if a claim needs to be logged onto your OSHA logs or not.

3. **Immediate Trend Reporting**: Because automated claims systems enable you to track claim details, you can now instantly download reports that enable you to pinpoint trends that are costing your company money. The bar charts below give you an idea of what can be tracked in today's claims management systems.

Accidents Waiting to Happen

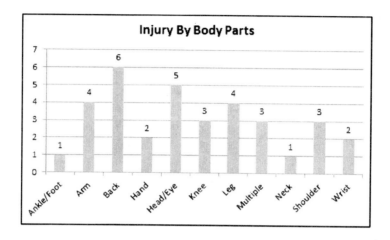

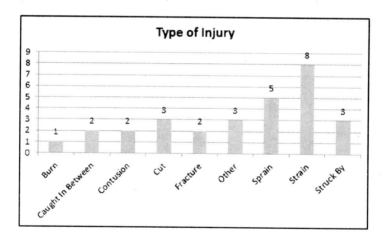

Accidents Waiting to Happen

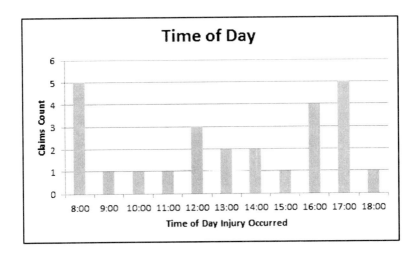

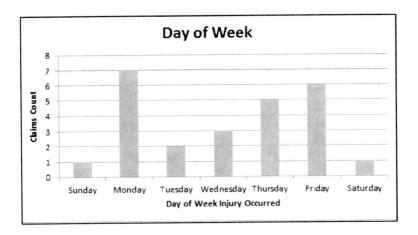

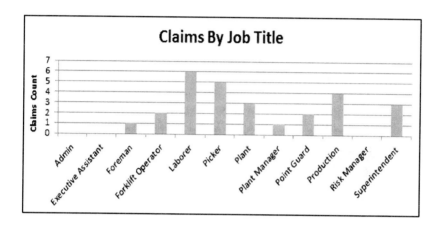

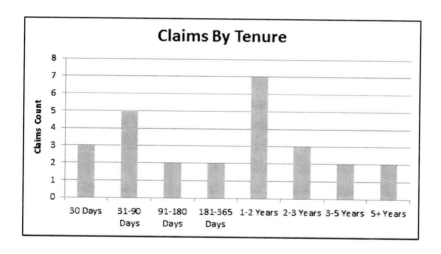

1. **Chronological Storage**: Companies with multiple locations and a number of claims to track, will especially benefit from having a system in which all claim activities can be easily organized and viewed in chronological order. With all the paperwork that dribbles in at different times of the day, week, or month, you can easily create notes or scan and attach documentation as you receive it to each respective file.

2. **Communication:** Good communication with your carrier adjuster(s) is one of the biggest factors impacting the effectiveness of your process. Your broker can set up a system to upload automatically the adjuster's email and phone number for any given claim. Rather than having to hunt for your adjuster's contact information; with the click of a button, you can automatically send them an email, with attachments, from your claims portal or you can call them at your convenience.

3. **Automatic triggers**: Effective claims management means being proactive in working with your carrier's adjuster when serious claim issues arise. In chapter 15, we will address what are known as "Red-Flag indicators." When submitting your claim to the insurance carrier, if red flag indicators are present, an automatic email report goes out to your broker to make sure your claim gets "special handling." Dealing with problem issues upfront is a secret ingredient to keeping your claim costs from spiraling out of control.

4. **Suspense Systems**: In chapter 15, we will talk about getting all-important documentation into the hands of the carrier's adjuster on a timely basis. Doing so helps

adjusters retool their time to focus their efforts on cost-saving activities rather than wasting clerical time requesting and following up on needed paperwork. Look for claims systems with built-in suspense capabilities that remind you of paperwork that still needs to be processed. With automatic reminders in place, claim activities will not fall through the cracks -- and cost you money down the road.

Reality check

Before we get to the "PX4" process, let's do a reality check about what lies ahead in the months and years to come. Why? In the next chapter, as we'll see, it's wise to be prepared for what's ahead, because history has a way of repeating itself.

*"Never leave that till tomorrow
which you can do today."*

~Benjamin Franklin

Chapter 9:

History Repeats Itself

Zürich Insurance Company published an article, "Recession, Recovery, and Your Workers' Compensation," which explains that after every recession, two things have happened every time:

1. Companies gradually begin to rehire, and
2. Workers' compensation claims always increase.

Through the years, history has repeated itself, and these two situations have occurred with regularity. The article asks a key question: are you properly positioned and prepared as the economy improves?

Do you have good Human Resource policies and procedures in place? How are your hiring practices? What tools are you using to stay organized with all the responsibilities you face on a daily basis?

This article is so important I sought and received permission to reprint it.

"Recession, Recovery, and Your Workers' Compensation"

As the economy slowly recovers, the various impacts of the worst economic downturn since the great depression became clearer. According to the National Bureau of Economic Research, a private panel of economists, which is now widely known as the "Great Recession," began in December 2007 and ended in June 2009, making it the longest recession since World War II. Hundreds of trillions of dollars of wealth was destroyed, thousands of companies shut their doors and millions of Americans lost their jobs. Though the recession has been declared over, recovery is agonizingly slow.

Recession impacts workers' comp claims

The recession touched almost every aspect of operations for companies across America, including risk management and insurance. One area that was especially affected was workers' compensation. Because of layoffs, many companies saw their workers' compensation premiums fall. The recession also had an impact on workers' compensation claims. Several factors combined reduced, on average, the number of workers' compensation claims. The National Council on Compensation Insurance, Inc (NCCI) statistics shows that workers' compensation claim frequency fell 4% in 2009. As prosperity returns and companies begin to hire again, they need to take steps to ensure that workers' compensation losses do not suddenly surge, which has happened during prior periods of economic recovery.

The Recession

Since workers' compensation costs are directly related to payroll, it is important to understand the impact of the recession on employment and how the economic and labor landscape has changed. With the unemployment rate still hovering around 10%, it is clear that many employers have had to make difficult decisions. Companies have had to reduce headcount, do more with less and run operations that are more efficient. The impact of these decisions on workers' compensation costs runs deeper than may at first be obvious.

History tends to repeat itself and what has happened in previous recessions is holding true for this one as well. The most viable impact for employers is the reduction of premium due to lower payrolls, and the correlation of these reduced payrolls with the frequency of claims. Fewer employees, not surprisingly, translate into fewer claims. But the impact goes much further than a proportional reduction of claims as the workforce shrinks. Some factors lead to even greater reduction in claim frequency as well as lower claim severity, while others push in the other direction and contribute to an increase in both frequency and severity of workers' compensation claims.

When employees decide to cut costs by reducing their workforce, they often do so by eliminating the less experienced and less skilled workers first. They want to maintain the best employees for when business turns around, and they feel their more experienced employees can handle a bigger burden before they have to begin to hire new people. Despite a possible negative effect due to increased fatigue on an aging workforce, experience has shown this situation leads to a decline in the frequency of workers' compensation claims. Beyond the fact that there are fewer employees, the employees who remain on staff often are more experienced, better trained and usually more loyal. US Bureau of Labor Statistics data show that more experienced employees have fewer and less severe workers' compensation claims: at normal employment levels, workers with less than one year of experience with an employer represent 25% of the workforce, yet have 34% of the lost time claims and costs. Statistics from Zürich indicate that workers with less than one year of experience represent 38% of lost time claims and 43% of lost time claim costs.

Business owners and managers also should be aware that, with the continued high unemployment rates and the extended length of time it takes an unemployed worker to find a new job, some employees may be incentivized to drag out workers' compensation payments.

The phenomenon of malingering, which is always a concern for employers and insurance companies, becomes more prevalent in a recession.

During uncertain times, some injured workers are more likely to exaggerate their illnesses and injuries so they can stay out for extended periods. If they fear when they return to work they are at risk of being terminated, they may do what they can to remain out on workers' compensation as long as possible.

The Recovery

In the early stages of an economic recovery, employers have been reluctant to increase their labor forces. They are relying on their current employees to meet the increased production needs by working longer hours. Because the recovery thus far has not created many jobs, it has been coined as the "jobless recovery."

Extended unemployment also means that an aging workforce, once they return to work, likely will work past retirement age because of lost retirement funds and savings. So what does all this mean for employers when the economy is in full recovery and hiring picks up?

Same stuff, different day

As previously noted, history tends to repeat itself. In prior recoveries, when employers increased their workforce to meet the increased demand for products and services, the number of workers' compensation claims tended to rise as well. New and less experienced employees were found to be significantly more likely to become injured. More experienced employees tended to search for other employment opportunities as compensation begins to take priority over job security. This resulted in a larger, less experienced workforce performing job duties they were neither qualified for nor trained in.

The same concerns remain this time around. Not only will businesses be hiring less experienced people, they will also deal with an aging workforce to fill jobs that require new skills. The combination could be a serious cause of concern for employers.

As was seen in previous recoveries, this could create real potential for increased claims activity that would result in much higher insurance costs.

Employers need to keep in mind that deteriorating claims experience in the short-term might impact their workers' compensation premiums for years to come. Increased workers' compensation claim costs in 2011 and 2012 would impact Experience Modification factors in 2013, 2014 and 2015, which can lead to higher premiums in those years. It is important that businesses learn from the past and develop strategies to help minimize the potential impact that the economic recovery can have on their workers' compensation costs.

The Solution

In order to keep up with the demand for goods and services during the recovery, there is no way around hiring new and inexperienced people. But as we have seen, there is a relationship between an increase in workers' compensation claims and new employees. If businesses want to reduce workplace injuries and keep Worker's Compensation premiums to a minimum, they need to look at the potential causes of claims with new employees and develop a strategy to help reduce and minimize the frequency and severity of these claims.

According to a study by Zürich, the main factors that contribute to an increase in claims with employees on the job for less than one year are:

- Inappropriate job placement,
- Lack of appropriate orientation and training,
- Unfamiliarity with hazards of the workplace or specific operation of equipment,
- Tendency to take shortcuts with safety procedures to complete tasks on time, and
- Hesitancy to ask for help or information needed to work safely.

Some best practices to help minimize the potential impact that the economic recovery can have on workers' compensation costs include:

- Use current job analysis to attract qualified candidates for each job,
- Insist that recruiting and hiring practices comply with current regulations,
- Apply pre-placement and post-offer testing to validate new hire qualifications,
- Provide relevant training that emphasizes worker and workplace safety, and
- Consider tenure of claimants in evaluating lost time claims to identify corrective action.

Start planning now

Amid continuing economic uncertainty, one thing is certain. It will be a while before the economy gains enough momentum that employers will feel comfortable hiring large numbers of new employees. However, employers should not wait until hiring picks up and business is booming to begin planning how they will keep their workers' compensation costs under control during the economic recovery.

While some increase in workers' compensation claims may be inevitable during the recovery, employers can reduce workplace injuries and control workers' compensation costs through a combination of careful hiring practices, training and heightened loss control activities.

Managing workers' compensation costs requires foresight, preparation and execution, but business owners and managers do not have to go it alone. Help should be available from insurance brokers and workers' compensation insurers.

Note: Josh Bradford of Advisen Ltd. wrote this article in October 2010 for Zurich in North America. The information in this article was obtained from sources believed to be reliable and is for informational purposes only. Any and all information contained herein is not intended to constitute legal advice and accordingly, you should consult with your own attorneys when developing programs and policies. Zurich does not guarantee the accuracy of this information or any results and further assume no liability in connection with this article. The article is reproduced by Rick Dalrymple with permission from Advisen and Zurich in North America.

"It is not whether you get knocked down;

it is whether you get up."

~Vince Lombardi

SECTION II

THE PROCESS

Chapter 10:

RiskScore®

Do you know your Risk-Score ?

CREDIT SCORE

720

Do you want lower insurance costs?

If you answered a resounding "YES," let me ask you a second question. Do you know your company's *RiskScore®*?

If your answer is "no", or you are not sure, don't worry. I am going to show you how you can easily find out what your *RiskScore®* is.

This is important, because your *RiskScore®* holds a key to reducing your company's insurance costs. More on this below.

Increases in workers' comp costs

Let's start with a basic assumption: businesses will see increases in costs with their workers' compensation coverage. In several states, employers have already seen continuous yearly rate increases in 2011, 2012, and 2013. As you know, medical costs are a major component of workers' compensation pricing. As medical costs continue to rise, it is critical for businesses to insulate themselves with sound operational procedures.

There's another reason, too. As the United States emerges from the Great Recession, expect another dangerous trend to negatively impact businesses in the coming years:

Insurance rates will rise at a more rapid pace!

There are several reasons for this:

1. Insurance companies' investment income has been low in recent years and has not kept pace with industry losses.

2. According to NBC News, 2011 will go down in history as the costliest year ever for insurance companies. The claims they paid due to natural disasters totaled over $265 billion. Carriers will recoup these losses by raising rates. (footnote: NBCNews.com. 7/12/11 "2011 Already Costliest Year for Natural Disasters") http://www.msnbc.msn.com/id/43727793/ns/world_news-world_environment/t/already-costliest-year-natural-disasters#.UMoFPG_Acuc

3. Increasing loss ratios, coupled with inadequate premiums, forces carriers to increase rates to maintain profitability.

When investment income fails to offset claim reserves, the outcome is to increase consumers' insurance rates.

Are you Best in Class?

So, it's obvious for several reasons rates will rise in the short-term. How can you best position your business and cushion it from these anticipated premium rate increases and remain profitable? The answer lies in a company's ability to be viewed as "Best in Class" by insurance company underwriters.

Underwriters are the people responsible for pricing your account. The more comfortable they are with what your agent submits, the better pricing you are likely to receive. Businesses that are viewed as "Best in Class" typically qualify for larger discounts and better programs. They consequently receive lower insurance premiums than their peers. In order for a company to qualify as "Best in Class," they typically must have low loss ratios (under 25%) and have policies and procedures in place to reduce their claims, business risk and operational costs.

If you want better pricing on your next insurance renewal, it is very important that you have a good understanding of how your company is being represented in the marketplace. Let me ask you this question. When was the last time you saw the submission that was used by your agent to represent you in the marketplace? I strongly recommend taking a look.

More times than not, brokers send "Accord Form" applications and copies of your loss run (also known as your claims history reports) to insurance company underwriters.

Now imagine submitting a package that contains the following information on your company:

1. Photographs
2. A narrative summary that articulates your "success" story as a best-in-class organization and includes safety steps the company is taking to mitigate risk.
3. Loss-ratio summaries
4. A copy of your company's safety material

The Rest of the Story

Every day underwriters process wave after wave of agent submissions. They are busy people just like you, and have to decide which accounts to spend their time on. The typical bland, generic submissions don't give underwriters enough information to get a "feel" for your company.

Now imagine your company's submission catching the attention of an insurance underwriter. It includes color photographs of your location that document key parts of your application. Use photos to illustrate clearly the good housekeeping at your facility, the security system you have in place, the fence around your property, and the safety equipment you use. A little color goes a long way toward getting your company to stand out from the crowd.

In your narrative summary, map out your company's history as a success story. More important, articulate the many steps your company has taken to promote safety and prevent future losses. Your company may have had some unfortunate claims in the past that caused your loss ratios to increase. Underwriters appreciate a company's honesty about addressing past claim issues. They want assurance you have taken proactive steps to mitigate future claim occurrences.

When underwriters receive your loss runs from brokers, they generally receive pages and pages of information that require a lot of time to sort through in an effort to determine your claim-total results. Instead, save them time. They love to see all that claims data summarized so they can more quickly assess whether you meet their underwriting guidelines.

Finally, email an electronic version of your company's safety material to your agent, who can use that information to paint a better picture about your company.

Last years' paperwork

Bottom line: if you want better pricing at your next renewal, make sure your submission stands out. Here is another item to add to your "TO DO" list. Contact your agent 4 to 5 months before your renewal date. Ask for a copy of the paperwork submitted last year to represent your company to the marketplace. How does it look to you?

As I said earlier, one key to profitability and lower insurance rates, is knowing your company's *RiskScore®*. This tool can be used to have better discussions with insurance company underwriters. In the financial world, homeowners understand that mortgage underwriters look at your credit score when providing mortgage interest rates. When applicants have a good-to-high credit score, they typically receive lower mortgage rates, right?

The same holds true in the insurance world.

A good-to-high" *RiskScore®* usually translates into lower insurance rates and lower insurance premiums. In order to maximize the credits and discounts your company qualifies for, complete a risk assessment and calculate your *RiskScore®*.

You may not realize this yet, but your *RiskScore®* can become the benchmark from which to construct a roadmap for changes that your company desires to make, to improve your position with the underwriting community.

Fast-track:

If you are interested in knowing your company's *RiskScore®* without further delay, go to www.WhatsMyRiskScore.com to begin the process.

Meanwhile, let me explain in more detail …

What *RiskScore®* Represents and How to Use It to Your Advantage.

Don't be surprised if your agent or broker is not familiar with *RiskScore®*. Many are not.

RiskScore® represents how you compare with your peer group in the administration of their workers' compensation program when considering industry Best Practices. It brings your strengths as a company to light, and shows where your opportunities for improvement exist, (as it relates to reducing your risk).

Calculating your *RiskScore®* begins by answering a series of questions that relate to your policies and procedures. The more written policies and procedures in place, the higher your *RiskScore®*.

Note: Be honest with your answers, because you may be asked to produce the evidence.

Similar to a credit score, a perfect *RiskScore*® is 850. At this point, your goal should be to begin deploying those policies and procedures that will increase your score.

But get this …underwriters are more interested in knowing what your company is doing to prevent losses.

In other words, it is less important to tell your carrier your *RiskScore*® number than to articulate clearly how your company handles various aspects of workers' compensation administration.

Calculating your *RiskScore*® is easy. It's less easy to implement critical procedures to run a more effective workers' comp program.

Let's take a look at "why" some procedures are critical. When you understand why you should take certain steps and you communicate their importance across the organization, it's a lot easier to get the buy-in you need from your staff.

The great thing about an *RiskScore*® is that it provides a benchmark that lets you know where your company stands today. When you take steps to improve your processes, your *RiskScore*® increases. I recommend going through the *RiskScore*® process on an annual basis to measure your improvement, and reinforce what should be in place from an operational standpoint.

The *RiskScore*® process should involve C-level executives, as well as HR and administration team members, because workers' compensation administration impacts various levels throughout your organization.

CEOs, CFOs or COOs need to pay attention to *RiskScore*® as a leading indicator because of its impact on the profitability of your company. I often see *RiskScores*® with a 25% variance in the ultimate score within the same company, and that is okay -- at least initially. What's important here is that everyone is on the same page about what best practices are. Then management is in a better position to communicate and/or change company policy in a systematic and organized way. Your ultimate goal is that the *RiskScore*® be the same in all company departments.

Is everyone in your boat rowing in the same direction?

The *RiskScore*® process has been found to be very appealing to multi-state/location companies who want greater consistency of operations within their organizations. It is much easier to drive positive results when everyone in your boat is rowing in the same direction.

Bottom line, the more comfortable an underwriter is with your company's application and its risk-mitigation plans, the easier it is to trust you will be a profitable policyholder. Consequently, you are more likely to receive preferred programs and pricing considerations. The *RiskScore*® process creates a systematic way to track your company's actions to reduce your operating costs and increase your profitability.

See your workers' comp claims drop

Knowing your *RiskScore*® is just the beginning. Some companies that have gone through the *RiskScore*® process have ultimately seen their workers' compensation claims drop by over 62%, while the severity of their claims fell over 21%. As we discussed earlier, this process has had a remarkable impact.

For more information, go to www.WhatsMyRiskScore.com.

In the next chapter

You will learn about a system called the "PX4" process, which has been extremely successful in helping small, medium, and large companies increase their profitability.

"The elevator to success is out of order. You'll have to use the stairs…One step at a time."

~Joe Girard

Chapter 11:

The "PX4" Process

At the heart of any successful endeavor, there is usually a plan. If one of your goals as a company is to increase your profitability, a successful program, called the "PX4" Process, has proven its ability to drive positive results for companies of all sizes.

The material you are about to read was created from thousands of hours of time-tested, industry accepted practices that are a part of any "Best Practices" organization. I am proud to say that not only is this an attorney-approved system, the "PX4" process has been endorsed by several leading insurance carriers in the United States.

You could spend months trying to compile the thought leadership needed to create the system you are about to learn, but fortunately for you, it has been distilled into an easy-to-understand set of business practices that will serve your company well in the years to come. My goal is to provide you with practical policies and procedures that you can begin implementing today.

Some of the material will be basic in nature, and some will be more advanced due to the complex nature of workers' compensation administration. I always recommend that businesses seek the advice of legal counsel. I highly recommend you have contact information for an expert workman's comp attorney, whose practice is to assist employers in mitigating legal issues, and help bring cases to a close. I also recommend that you have a good labor law attorney, who can help you with many of the HR (Human Resource) related protocols for employee administration.

Impact on your bottom line

When implementing the many policies and procedures of a successful workers' comp program, some steps are more critical than others are. Companies that have gone through the *RiskScore®* process (www.WhatsMyRiskScore.com), quickly learn that some procedures can easily be implemented, and most all will have a big and positive impact on their bottom line. A couple of quick examples in the next few chapters include your use of *medical questionnaires* and *integrity testing*. You will learn why those items are of particular importance.

Successful workers' comp program

Creating and managing a successful workers' compensation program has proven to have the following outcomes on companies, whatever their industry or location:

1. Increased profitability

2. Lower operating expenses

3. Streamlined efficiency

4. Had the effect of increased sales

5. Reduced business risk / fewer employee lawsuits

6. Fewer and lower-cost workers' comp claims

7. Increased competitiveness in the marketplace

In other words, the positive outcomes of adopting the "PX4" process are seen company-wide. My goal is to show you why each step is so important to deploy. (I don't know about you, but I always want to understand "why" I should do certain things.)

So let's get started.

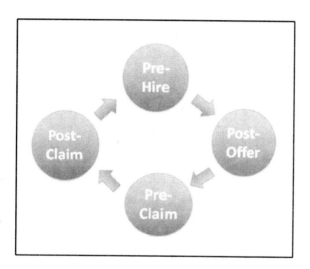

The "PX4" process focuses on these key areas:

> ➢ Pre-Hire
> ➢ Post-Offer
> ➢ Pre-Claim
> ➢ Post-Claim

I will provide details in each of these areas in subsequent chapters. The "PX4" process encompasses a holistic approach that involves not only the proper management of claims themselves, but just as important, an overview of proper HR procedures that should be in place in order to reduce your risk of having claims to begin with.

Pre-Hire:

After more than 30 years in practice, I know the best place to start reducing the cost and number of claims is in the Pre-Hire process. Surprised? How you hire and who you hire is huge in driving better results in workers' compensation.

Post-Offer:

As the economy improves, it is dangerous to hire people without having good protocols in place to reduce your risk. In this step, there are some very simple, yet very important procedures to make sure you "on-board" your new hires the right way.

Pre-Claim:

As you learn more about this program, you will find some policies and procedures time-consuming to implement. However, some policies and procedures can be easily tailored to your company. It could take a while to pull all the necessary material together. This is where you will evaluate the capabilities and turnkey services you get from your current broker, and seek help if needed.

Implement your policies

You may have the most up to date three ring binders in your filing cabinet that contain every policy and procedure you need to have in place, mapped out perfectly to fit your company. However, that manual will do you no good unless you implement what's inside it.

Post-Claim:

In this stage, we examine the procedures and checklists to follow "after" a claim occurs. It's highly unlikely you will have zero claims in the future. When you do have a claim, you'll be glad you have a system that will keep you organized and protect your profit margins.

Yours may be one of those rare companies that has not had a claim in years. Unfortunately, I have seen companies let their guard down thinking they had correct business procedures in place, only to get broadsided by an issue they did not see coming.

When you receive your next claim, I want you armed with knowledge to get the necessary materials to the adjusters within just a few days. Having your paperwork in order at the beginning of a claim can be critical to your profitability.

In the next chapter

The journey continues with Step One, the Pre-Hire process. Each process will build upon the others. Take time to review each step.

And, if you really get stuck....no worries (☺). I am just a phone call away if you have questions. I can be reached at (321) 578-7559.

"The secret to getting started is breaking your complex, overwhelming tasks into small manageable tasks, and then starting on the first one."

~Mark Twain

Chapter 12:

Pre-Hire Process

In the previous chapter, I outlined a system called a "PX4" process, which has been very successful in driving positive results for companies in the management of their workers' compensation program.

Step 1: The Pre-Hire process

Did you know there is a direct correlation between the effectiveness of your hiring process and the claims that your company sustains? Consequently, it is crucial to examine your hiring practices.

> There is a direct correlation between the effectiveness of your hiring process and claims your company sustains.

What does your hiring process look like these days?

Do you have a watertight process in place, or have you gotten rusty in the last few years simply because you have not done much hiring? Do your employee applications include the latest fraud statements?

Understand up front, that if you hire the wrong employees, or you don't have good systems in place once you bring them on board,

> **If you end up hiring the wrong employees, ...your company will lose money.**

your company will lose money. Guaranteed. The beginning of any successful workers' compensation program starts with making sure you hire the right people. After letting your new employee on "your bus," make sure you get them in their proper seat.

Key areas to consider during the Pre-Hire process:

1. Hiring checklist
2. Interview questions
3. Employee testing
4. Reference checks
5. Written job descriptions
6. Background checks

Let's look at each of these in turn.

Hiring Checklist

Create a hiring checklist that maps out the activities that need to be accomplished when bringing on a new employee, in order to stay organized and to avoid important steps falling through the cracks. Even though all companies are unique and each has different needs, in the HR-arena, companies share a lot in common, whether they are large or small.

Examples of important HR items that include:

1. Conduct Post-offer/Pre-hire physicals
2. Verify applicant's background including
    a. Department of motor vehicle records (MVR)

    b. Criminal background checks

    c. Credit reports

    d. Verify gaps in employment

3. Conduct technical skills testing

4. Conduct Pre-hire profiling assessments (Integrity Testing)

5. Provide new hire orientation (including safety training)

6. Conduct consistent "on boarding" meetings with new hires

Involve a potential new hire's co-workers in the interview process. Make sure the interview process is not a singular event (1-2 hour interview). Interview candidates more than once, at different times of the day, and in different environments to get a better sense what the employee is all about.

Your new motto

Make "Always Be Recruiting" your HR motto. Start looking for candidates to fill a position before the need arises. Always have a pipeline of qualified candidates. Too often, employers scramble quickly and put feelers out for potential hires, and rush to fill a position.

Have you had an employee get an attorney for their workers' compensation injury? Once you bring a new hire on board, that new employee can "own" you. If you have ever experienced an employee whom you felt was faking a workers' comp injury, was having absentee issues, or was disruptive to the productivity of your company, you know what I am talking about.

Slow to hire

Vigilance in the hiring process will save you many headaches and lost profits. Smart companies are slow to hire because they know employee turnover is costly and the expense of an employee lawsuit can be damaging to their bottom line.

Interview Questions

At the heart of any good interview process is the art of asking high-quality interview questions that will draw out answers from a candidate that help you pick the right employee for the job.

Ask "behavioral-based" questions. Ask questions that relate to the skills needed to be successful in the position, and allow candidates to demonstrate whether they possess those necessary attributes.

Author, Bob Norton, created a list of *"The 16 Best and Most Revealing Interview Questions"* you should ask candidates. For a copy of this information, go to http://tiny.cc/glj9ow (www.clevelenterprises.com)

Employee Testing (Integrity Testing):

The Society for Human Resource Management (SHRM) published an article in June 2011 that shared results of the success companies were having in conducting "Integrity Tests" with job applicants. These companies saw a dramatic fall in the number and costs of their workers' compensation claims. Researchers say that pre-employment screening, using "Integrity Testing," provides employers with reliable tools that predict undesirable behaviors in potential job candidates. These tests identify candidates who have blurred the lines between right and wrong behavior, and suffer from an "entitlement attitude."

One company in the article mentions Merchants Information Solutions Inc. in Phoenix, Arizona. (www.merchantsInfo.com) Behavioral assessments have proven very effective in identifying candidates in four high-risk behavioral areas:

1. Theft
2. Substance Abuse
3. Hostility
4. Faking

The test is often referred to as a "self-admitting" test, asking candidates about behaviors and practices identified as counter-productive to the work environment. A candidate found to be "High Risk" in any of these categories is considered a "Non-Qualified" candidate, and should not be invited to move forward in the hiring process.

By eliminating high-risk candidates with behavior issues, you are less likely to have false or exaggerated workers' comp claims filed against your company.

Reduction in works comp losses

Several industries, including construction, manufacturing, staffing, and retail, have shown an average of a 63% reduction in workers' comp losses after implementing Integrity Testing as part of their hiring process. These companies also enjoyed a 21% reduction in the severity of claims filed. To summarize, those candidates who pass an Integrity Test are less likely to file a claim, and when they do file a claim, it will be for a lower amount. These individuals follow doctor's orders and tend to return to work sooner.

Other benefits associated with the use of Integrity Testing in hiring:

- Improved profitability
- Lower turnover
- Decreased absenteeism
- Higher company morale
- Reduced theft
- Lower workplace violence

Integrity Testing is one of the few tools available that allows employers to assess a candidate's current state of mind.

Written Job Descriptions

In the Pre-hire process, it is critical to maintain current written job descriptions for all your employees' positions. Specifically, it is best if your job descriptions comply with the Americans with Disability Act (ADA).

Here is why written job descriptions are so important:

1. They keep you from asking the "wrong" questions during an interview (questions that do not relate to the job at hand), which could set you up for a discrimination lawsuit.
2. They are an effective tool doctors use to get injured employees back to work quicker after an accident.

I will discuss more about job descriptions in a later chapter when I discuss something called a "Return to Work" program.

To get more information on written job descriptions, visit O-Net Resource Center (www.onetcenter.org) for a wealth of information on this topic.

Background Checks

Background checks have been a mainstay of many businesses for years. I trust that before you bring on any new hire, you perform your due diligence on candidates by doing a background check.

I've listed three companies as resources below. You may want to review and compare the rates you currently pay for this important service:

1. First Advantage (www.FADV.com)
2. Edge Information Management (www.edgeinformation.com)
3. National Crime Search (www.nationalcrimesearch.com)

Who knows, you could save money and get better services too.

Employment Assessment Tools

As I'm sure you understand, the stakes are high in hiring. Make sure you hire the right person for your business needs. Ron Adler, a noted expert in the field of human resources and labor law, has created some helpful tools and worksheets that may assist you. He's given his permission to share these ideas with you.

The first of many tools to assist employers is a questionnaire known as the Recruitment, Selection, and Hiring Process Profile™ (RSH). This questionnaire is an easy checklist to evaluate your RSH process. For a copy, go to http://tiny.cc/xwkxrw.

Components of an HR audit process

Another useful tool is ELLA™ (Employment- Labor Law Audit) HR Audit Worksheet™, which maps out five critical components of an HR audit process.

ELLA™ is the nation's leading HR auditing and employment practices liability risk assessment tool. It enables you to access your strengths and weaknesses, and prioritize the action items you want to address. For a copy of the worksheet, go to http://tiny.cc/tdjxrw.

The Recruitment, Selection, and Hiring (RSH) process is about the search for talent that adds value, makes your organization more competitive, and helps you achieve your business objectives. Your RSH practices will affect revenue generation, productivity, customer relations, market share, profitability, risk exposure, and even long-term survival. CEOs regularly rank "new hire quality" as the most important HR measurement.

In today's global economy, the recruitment, selection, and hiring process must address both short-term and long-term organizational needs. These activities are influenced and shaped by economic, budgetary, technological, social, demographic, and legal regulatory forces. The profile tools referenced above review various aspects of your organization's RSH process, which can help you:

1. Assess strengths and weaknesses of your hiring process
2. Increase the value of your human capital
3. Enhance hiring outcomes, and
4. Reduce your exposure to human capital risks and employment related liabilities

In the next chapter

I will review the second step in the "PX4" process called the Post-Offer step. I focus on what you should be doing after you offer someone a job. "On-Boarding" describes a process in which we will look at how you bring someone on board, and what you do with him or her after you have offered them a job.

"The greater danger lies not in setting our aim too high and failing short; but in setting our aim too low, and achieving our mark."

~Michelangelo

Chapter 13:

Post-Offer Process

Once you complete Step One, Pre-Hire, you are ready to make an offer.

After the job offer

Step Two of the "PX4" process is called the "Post-Offer" step. This step addresses what you should be doing after you have offered someone a job.

Does your company use the following documents?

1. Post-offer Health Questionnaire
2. Conditional Offer of Employment Letter

If you don't use these two documents, the impact on your company could be huge and negative. While there are some jurisdictional differences throughout the United States in how certain aspects of hiring protocols are viewed, it is nonetheless very important. Let me explain.

As any HR professional will tell you, never ask health questions of an applicant during the pre-hire interview process. (If you do, you had better have a labor law attorney on your speed dial, because it's only a matter of time before you get hit with a discrimination lawsuit.)

Bottom line

After you offer your candidate a job, then, and only then, are you able to request that your new hire complete a medical health questionnaire.

For obvious reasons, it would be great if your Post-offer health questionnaire were bilingual, but more importantly, does it contain the latest fraud statement acceptable under today's statutes? (http://tiny.cc/flhxrw)

Post-offer health questionnaires are important if a candidate was "less than truthful" in their employment paperwork, and advised you they had had no previous workers' comp injuries (when in fact they had), proper documentation will enable your insurance company to deny workers' compensation benefits, saving your company a lot of lost profits.

A case in point

Let's look at an example. A manufacturing company failed to put good hiring practices in place. An open position was quickly filled without documentation of the new employee's back surgery three months prior. Would you be surprised to hear that within two weeks of hiring, the employees back was reinjured; generating medical bills that ultimately totaled $76,178?

Based upon the net-profit margin of 3.5%, the company needed an additional $2,158,722 in sales to make up for this loss.

There are two issues involved here. Let's say the employee was truthful and acknowledged his prior back injury. Assessments would need to be made to determine whether the employee was capable of doing the job, or do the job with reasonable accommodations. This is where a good written job description proves valuable, by articulating the exact job duties and physical capabilities required.

Case law

If, however, an applicant is less than truthful on the application, case law has been established that enables an insurance company to deny the claim.

Two schools of thought

Some HR professionals are uncomfortable using Post-offer health questionnaires in the hiring process. They prefer not to know about any pre-existing conditions, because if they do, they open themselves up to the added expense of financially having to make "reasonable accommodations" for the potential hire.

Because of case law, most HR professionals and attorneys subscribe to the practice of using post-offer health questionnaires. Most want applicants to provide full disclosure of information that might impact their eligibility for the job offered.

Key court case

Martin Company *versus* Carpenter (132 So.2d 400 (1961) has become statute and gives your carrier the ability to deny workers' compensation benefits, if it is determined that an applicant was less than truthful with the information provided during the hiring process. For more information on this case, go to http://tiny.cc/3cl9ow.

Another important point to keep in mind regarding the administration of Post-offer health questionnaires is to make sure the medical questionnaires are kept separate and confidential from your other employee new hire package material. They should be filed in a locked cabinet away from your other HR material in order to comply with HIPPA (Health Insurance Portability & Accountability Act of 1996) regulations.

Conditional offer of employment letter

In essence, a "Conditional Offer of Employment letter", buys employers some extra time to check out an applicant's background before formally putting them to work. The letter lets your potential new hire know your company is seriously interested and intends to hire them, but you are completing your due diligence before formalizing your offer. For a sample copy of a Conditional Offer of Employment letter, go to http://tiny.cc/0wk9ow .

It is never a good practice to hire someone today, and put them on the job tomorrow. You need to thoroughly check the applicant out and make sure they are a good fit for your company. Every business is unique. You may have different hiring requirements than your competitor down the street. Some may want extra time to conduct pre-employment physicals or integrity testing, where as some will do other assessments such as job skills qualifications or drug testing.

In some states, you can go on government websites and check if the applicant has filed previous workers' compensation claims.

Wouldn't you like to know if a new applicant has filed numerous workers' comp claims before joining your company?

Knowledge is power and money saved

Knowing this information, in addition to what they disclosed on the Post-offer health questionnaire could impact your hiring decision....right? Clearly when situations like this arise, please know that you are in dangerous territory, and you may want to seek the advice of a labor law attorney to help guide you on matters like this, because you do not want to be facing a potential discrimination lawsuit.

The other point to remember, post-offer, is to be sure you have a good "on boarding" process.

On-boarding

Does your company have a thorough company orientation checklist to help you stay on top of everything that needs to be completed and discussed with your new hire?

Are new employees provided with proper safety information and training, as well as their job description? If your company has an organized training program, get your new hire started on training immediately.

In the next chapter

I will review the third step in the "PX4" process, called the Pre-Claim step. I will discuss the policies and procedures you should have in place before your company faces its next workers' compensation claim. Even if it's been a while, your company is not immune from claims. Having the right procedures in place reduces your company's risk when those claims occur.

"Expect the best. Prepare for the worst. Capitalize on what comes."

~Zig Ziglar

Chapter 14:

Pre-Claim Process

Step three of the "PX4" process addresses the policies and procedures you should have in place before your next workers' compensation claim.

Assume your new hire is in place. You can now turn your attention to increasing revenue and growing your business. Now is the time to conduct an evaluation audit to make sure you have policies and procedures in place that reduce your risk, as well as your operational costs.

Drug Free Work Place

A Drug-Free workplace program is one of the most important programs your company should have installed. If you are reading this book, you probably already have a drug-free workplace program. If your company does not have one in place yet, have it deployed at your earliest convenience.

There may be a financial incentive for having a drug-free workplace at your company. In some states, insurance companies provide an upfront discount.

For example, Arizona, South Carolina, and Florida companies receive a 5% upfront discount for having a drug-free workplace.

The "real" value

The "real" value of a drug-free workplace program at your company is not from upfront discounts you may receive. The real benefit comes from the protection it provides, leaving you better positioned to reduce your risk of claims and their associated costs. It has been said that drug users are five times more likely to file a claim than their non-drug-using counterparts.

Your insurance carrier has the opportunity to deny a claim if an employee tests positive to having drugs in their system at the time of the accident. A claim denial saves your company money from the financial impact of a drug related claim. Put on your "To Do" list to make sure your drug free workplace program has been validated and is up to date. You will find more information in the appendix on proper testing procedures and circumstances.

Easy jobs

If your company does not have a drug-free workplace program in place, you become the path of least resistance for those individuals trying to find a job. If your competition has a drug-free workplace program in place, which effectively screens out drug users, employees must find employment at a company without a drug-free workplace program.

Check your state regulations

State requirements differ on how to deploy an effective drug-free workplace program. Evaluate your program and make sure it complies with state requirements. Refer to the Appendix, page 210 for more details.

Temp-to-Perm hiring strategy

An often-overlooked strategy, hiring temporary employees before actually bringing them on full time, has been effective for many businesses. The worst thing you can do is rush to hire an employee you are not confident will be a long-term good fit for your company. Why not take the time to have an employee work with you for a few months, and get a chance to see their work ethic before actually offering them a permanent job?

This strategy may not be cost-effective for some industries and employees such as rank-and-file employees in the construction trades or in manufacturing. However, you may discover opportunities within your company where this approach works.

The point is, within the first several weeks or months of working with a new employee, you can get a good sense about whether they will be a productive employee for you. You do not want to hire the proverbial "Worm in the Apple" who is going to cost you money.

Return to Work Program

Having an effective Return to Work (R2W) program in place is a huge cost driver to your company. Let me give you an example. Let's say you have an employee who you suspect is trying to take advantage of the system and of your company by filing a workers' compensation claim. How you handle that claim will determine the ultimate cost of that claim to your company.

If, for example, one of your employees sustains injuries that cost over $7,000 in medical expenses; depending upon how you and your carrier adjuster handle this case, that claim will cost your company $7000, or as much as four times more than that, to the tune of $28,000.

How's that, you ask? In many states, in addition to you paying your workers' compensation premiums, you also pay back the dollar amount of claims your company sustained. Remember what we discussed earlier, your experience modification factor? Here is where that comes in to play. For an explanation of an experience modification factor, go to the Appendix, page 234.

You pay not only your premiums; you also repay the cost of your claims

I once talked with the CFO of a manufacturing company that paid over $125,000 for their workers' compensation policy. He thought claims were no big deal. When claims occurred he said, "That is why we have insurance, to pay these claims." He did not realize in the work comp system, you pay not only your premiums; you also repay the cost of your claims, by virtue of the increase to your experience modification factor.

If your company has a $10,000 workers' compensation claim, depending upon how that case evolves, you will continue to pay your premiums, but you will also eventually pay back $10,000 to the 'system' for that claim.

When I refer to the 'system,' I'm referring to whichever insurance carrier you are insured with at the time. An insurance carrier will charge you an increased amount of premium because of the increase to your experience mod factor. The question is, will that claim cost your company $10,000, or will it cost you $40,000?

You may ask how that happens. The answer lies in how your state calculates your experience modification factor. Once you let the carrier pay your employee's lost wages, in most states, you will have effectively quadrupled the cost of that claim because of how your state calculates your mod. In the next section, we will go into this further.

For now, to keep your claim costs from rising make sure your company has an effective Return to Work (R2W) program in place. When an employee is injured, if you can get that employee to return to work, you effectively reduce the cost of that claim. While every case is different, understand you will be doing your company and your employees a big favor by utilizing this strategy.

Getting employees back to work clearly benefits your company. It also supports the emotional well-being of your employee who is better served by getting them plugged back in at work. When they are away from work, you lose productivity.

For a sample copy of a Return to Work policy, feel free to go to: http://tiny.cc/nwlbpw.

Salary-in-lieu-of-comp strategy

Let's start with a note of caution. This advanced strategy should not be done without the help of an experienced claims consultant. Briefly, this strategy helps keep your claims cost from dramatically increasing. As I said before, the effect of allowing the insurance company to pay your employee for lost wages, has the effect of quadrupling the cost of your claim.

Of course, all claims are different, and need to be considered on a case-by-case basis. Here is how this process works. If your employee sustained an injury that could keep them out of work up to 21 days, your company can pay those lost wages rather than the insurance company. In most cases, you will want to pay a weekly rate of at least 80% of the employee's average weekly wages for the previous 13 weeks. Continue to pay a portion of lost wages until the employee gets back to work. Again, in doing so, you reduce the impact of this claim on your experience modification factor.

This strategy ties in perfectly with a return to work program. Each state calculates wages differently, so be sure you conform to your state's guidelines.

Modified Duty Work: using local charitable organizations

The minute the adjuster or employer receives the medical release for light-duty work, the cost savings clock is ticking. The benefits of early return to work are well documented and are common sense. People are creatures of habit, structure, and routine. Getting back to work produces a number of positive results, not the least of which is a reduction of the overall claim costs.

Case studies report that returning workers recuperate faster, incur lower medical costs, benefit psychologically, and will avoid the "out-of-work" syndrome. Returning to modified duty is shown to improve the employee's sense of self-worth and results in a more positive and productive experience, further reducing the chances of suffering an extended disability.

Shortened disability and reduced medical costs are what every risk manager hopes to achieve.

However, if you are a small employer, or have remote workers like long haul truck drivers, or manage the losses for a staffing company, returning the employee back to a light duty job may be impossible. One solution embraced by many employers currently is utilizing non-profit organizations to accommodate employee restrictions. In addition to the cost savings for employers, the benefits of this option include retaining experienced employees, potential tax advantages for paid volunteer work, and promoting a positive culture that all injured workers will be accommodated as quickly as possible.

Non-profit organizations welcome the variety of talents an injured employee can offer, whether the recovery period is a couple of weeks to several months. With over 2.3 million 501(c)(3) non-profit organizations nationwide, accommodating even the most limiting skill sets, language barriers, co-morbidity factors and irregular or part-time schedules is possible. Also, employee's medical or therapy appointments don't disrupt their operation as it could for the pre-injury employer.

Statistically, there is less than a .2% re-injury rate because the light duty activities assigned are designed to minimize risk and are monitored by the volunteer coordinator. These structured programs provide the employees with formal offer letters adhering to the statutory requirements of each state's jurisdiction. The process requires employees to sign an agreement specifying the terms of the assignment and acknowledge only performing work within their restrictions and adhering to all personnel policies of the pre-injury employer.

The agreement also requires the acknowledgement that the volunteer assignment is temporary and will not result in permanent employment with the non-profit agency. Companies such as ReEmployAbility, Inc. successfully place employees nationally through their "**Transition2Work** Program" utilizing an established network of non-profit partners. (www.reemployability.com)

Job Descriptions

When I talked earlier about making sure you had good policies and procedures in place, one of the items I was referring to was making sure you had good job descriptions on file for all your employees. They are very important and here is why.

Having good job descriptions on file enable an attending physician to determine and create proper transitional work the injured employee can do until they are able to fully come back to work without restrictions.

Bottom line, you want your employees back at work as quickly as possible. It's in your company's best interests, as well as the employee's. Arming the physician with this type of documentation is an important part of your return-to-work program.

Job Task Analysis (JTA)

After creating job descriptions for the various groupings of staff members you employ, you may want to consider a "job task analysis" for each group. This process allows you to determine scientifically the skills, tasks and areas of knowledge needed for the job.

The challenge in creating a JTA is coming up with a thorough list of tasks an employee is responsible for. Work with a firm able to validate any exam objectives, just in case you are legally challenged during the hiring process.

For more detailed explanation why job task analysis is important to deploy, please refer to the appendix on page 199.

Sign Off Sheets

As you see, much of the pre-claim process involves making sure that you have good policies and procedures in place before another claim is filed. From a procedural standpoint, it is always a good idea to have your employees sign an "acknowledge form" for all the most-important policies and procedures your company supports.

For example, have employees sign forms acknowledging they have read and understood your **safety manual**. Also, you want your new employees to know immediately upon hiring, that your company has a **Return to Work** program in place, and if they are ever injured, they know that you will find work for them.

Your employees should also know that you are serious about your **drug-free workplace** policy, and last but not least, use Post-offer **medical health questionnaires** in your hiring process.

Sample sign off sheets for drug free workplace, safety, and return-to-work programs are available in the appendix on page 237. A printable version of the sign off sheets can be retrieved by going to http://tiny.cc/q5q9ow.

*"When you come to the end of your rope,
tie a knot and hang on."*

~Franklin D. Roosevelt

Chapter 15:

Post-Claim Process

In this chapter, I will address some policies and procedures that should be in place and deployed *after* you have your next claim. Let's face it, it is not a matter of "if" you are going to have a claim, it is a matter of "when." For that next claim, develop a roadmap of what should be done to make certain your claim gets off on the right foot.

Written Accident Investigation forms

Let's start with something that may seem basic, but is a critical part of a successful claims process.

- What written documentation are you requiring after a claim occurs?

- Do you have an accident investigation form to document the facts of your losses? Is it a single page form or is it a multipage document that enables you to collect the needed level of detail?

- Who signs off on your documentation?

- Who is required to complete an accident investigation form? If you answered – "almost everyone," you are on the right track.

When an accident occurs, get a "written" description on what happened from each of the following individuals:

1. The injured employee
2. The injured employee's supervisors
3. Witnesses
4. Management

The number of employers who do not require written descriptions from injured employees amazes me.

Note: Depending upon the severity of the accident, it may not be practical for an injured employee to give you a written statement at the onset of the claim.

However, if their injuries were serious, and their condition has stabilized, get written documentation from the injured employee. Having this documentation on file clarifies and facilitates future discussions as the claim unfolds.

I will soon discuss "root cause" analysis questions that will supplement your investigation process to prevent future claims.

Where appropriate, be sure the injured employee's supervisors provide written descriptions of what they know about the claim. Supervisors play an important role in how safety is deployed within your company. Supervisors should be held accountable for the success of your safety program, and involving them actively in the claims investigation process is critical.

Witness statements

It is important to get statements from any witnesses who have seen the accident. When you request witness statements, get all contact information as well from the witnesses.

I have observed situations in the past, where companies failed to get witness names and contact information on the investigation form. In one case, when a jury trial was needed two years down the road, the company had no way to reach the witness who was willing to testify on their behalf.

Management should also keep written documentation on file, detailing their knowledge about the case. Management should be plugged in to all claims that occur, because once they understand that claims cost money, they will understand that every detail of a claim offers insight into finding ways to prevent future claims.

Red Flag Indicator questions

Make red flag indicator questions an integral part of your post-claim process. Here is why they are so important. By asking the right questions and having the appropriate responses on file, you arm the claims adjuster with important material that can help them mitigate the cost of your claim.

Employer plays key role in keeping costs down

What has been learned through the years is that approximately 70% of your success in keeping claims costs down rests on your shoulders as the employer, not the insurance company. Many employers tell me they rely on the insurance company for all the investigation leg work. As I shared earlier, insurance company adjusters are buried in paperwork. They may not have time to investigate thoroughly every claim.

You, the employer, are in a much better position to provide complete accident-investigation notes to the claim file in a timely manner. You also understand the chemistry of the case because you know the people involved.

Here are a few examples of red flag indicator questions:

1. Was the employee's job being eliminated?
2. Was this a disgruntled employee?
3. Were there any conflicting stories from the written statements that you acquired?
4. Did the employee refuse a post-accident drug test?
5. Was there a delay in the employee reporting the claim?

Answers to questions like these are valuable to an adjuster working the case.

Root cause analysis questions

Similar to red flag indicator questions, root cause analysis questions are also a critical part of your post-claim process.

Root cause analysis questions can help you identify trends in your company's claim activity. If trends occur, you are in a better position to address them quickly by providing safety training in the areas.

- Do you see a reoccurrence of the same type of injuries?

- Are you seeing a pattern of claims that specific training could help to reduce?

Here are some examples of some useful root cause analysis questions:

1. Was the employee properly trained for the job?
2. Was the injured employee following company safety rules?
3. Was the claim a result of unsafe working conditions?
4. What could have been done to avoid the accident?
5. Is there anything I can change to prevent future similar accidents?

Develop your own root cause analysis questions to fit the specific needs of your company.

Depending upon the level of the claim data you acquire, you can clearly map out analytics like:

1. What types of injuries are occurring?
2. What body parts are being injured?
3. Are your losses coming from your new or long-term employees?
4. What time of day or day of week are your losses occurring?

The question is the answer

Just by asking if the injured employee was following company safety rules and procedures can save your company a lot of lost profits and revenue. In some states, if an employee violates a company's safety rules (for example, not wearing a seatbelt when driving a company vehicle), carriers are permitted to reduce some of the benefits provided to the injured employee.

Imagine this scenario. One of your employees is involved in an automobile accident and sustains serious injuries that will keep them out of work for months. If the employee was not wearing a seatbelt, (a statutory requirement), some states allow carriers to reduce some of their benefits by up to 25%.

For a $100,000 claim, a carrier could reduce benefits by $25,000. That means you would have effectively prevented lost profits for your company. A company with a 5% net-profit margin would have to generate another $500,000 in sales to offset that extra $25,000 expenditure.

Fee Scheduled State

When a claim occurs, many states have set financial limits to what a medical provider can charge on worker's compensation injuries.

Some states are known as "fee scheduled states," meaning there are limits to what can be charged on specific workers' compensation injuries, based upon the injury code.

Imagine an employee broke a leg (simple break) and needs a cast. Whether the leg was broken at a family picnic or stepping off the ladder at work, determines the amount of the invoice that you get from the doctor's office or the hospital.

Injury codes and their corresponding payment allocation vary between states. Look at the chart on the next page to see examples of the amounts charged by a medical provider compared to the fee schedule. The savings can be significant.

Diagnosis / Diagnosis Code	Provider	Total Charges	Fee Schedule	Savings
3rd degree burn hand/arm #949.0	Hand Rehab	$140	$52	$88
Lumbar Strain #724.2	Walk-In Clinic	$150	$86	$64
Knee/Joint Pain #719.46	MRI	$200	$142	$58
Closed Fracture/Femur #821.20	Hospital	$86,387.05	$33,002.01	$53,385.04

Look at the hospital charge for treating a broken leg. The invoices from the hospital totaled over $86,000. Applying the fee schedule saved more than $53,000.

When sending an employee for medical treatment of an injury, make sure the medical provider knows that it is a workers' compensation claim. The pre-arranged fee schedule or network arrangement can make a significant difference in your cost.

Step by Step Procedures

Previously, I mentioned that you control the lion's share of your destiny on the number of claims you will incur, and how much your claims will cost.

I've already discussed that you don't want to rely solely on your insurance company or their adjusters in the management of your claims. If you blindly trust an adjuster to get all the facts and process everything on time, you will cost your company money.

Critical time frame

The first seven days of any claim are critical. That's why you should implement step-by-step procedures, ready to deploy after your next claim. Send the right documentation to the adjuster within the allotted time.

The law requires that within seven days of learning about any workplace injury, you must report the claim to the insurance company.

As quickly as you can, compile and forward to the adjuster the following information:

1. Accident investigation forms
2. Post-offer health questionnaire
3. Job description
4. Medical release
5. Red Flag indicator questions
6. Root Cause analysis questions
7. Wage statements

These seven items create an excellent base for an adjuster to use in mitigating the cost of your claims. I have already talked about most of this documentation, but items such as medical releases and wage statements may also be needed.

Medical release

At the onset of every claim, be sure medical releases are completed to ensure the adjuster has the injured employee's authorization to get all medical records they may need, including any from previous injuries.

Have you ever had an employee who has reinjured themselves from a prior injury at previous employers?

The adjuster needs the medical records that will explain details from the previous injury, and what medical treatment was provided. The adjuster will use these records to determine if the current injury is related to, or different from, the earlier injury.

Provide wage statements to the adjuster if you sense the employee will be out more than a week and could receive lost wage benefits. Obviously, wage statements are not needed for "medical only" claims.

A word of caution regarding wage statements; make sure they are completed accurately and promptly, if needed!

Too often, well-intentioned employers rush to get wage statement information to the adjuster, only to find that the financial information was incorrect. You can probably answer this next question quite easily. If the employee receives their first wage statement check, and it is less than what they were expecting, who do you think they will call? Let's hope they call you, rather than the local attorney they've seen advertised on TV continuously throughout the day.

Bottom line: make sure your wage statements are correct. If they are not, your employee could go to an attorney, increasing the cost of your claim by minimum of $10,000.

Each state is different, but in most states, insurance carriers have 14 to 21 days to determine the compensability of the claim. The carrier adjuster, once notified of the case, will go to work reviewing your paperwork and doing their own background investigation. They have systems that will help them determine if this injured employee has shown up in their database with prior workers' compensation injuries.

I started this chapter pointing out the importance of having good step-by-step procedures in place, and the need to get the proper documentation to the adjuster within the first seven days of the case. By getting the right documentation to the adjuster in a timely manner, you have effectively helped them become more effective in helping you mitigate your claim. If the adjuster has to waste time following up on clerical documentation, it costs your company money.

Nurse Triage

Nurse triage services have become very popular in recent years due to their ability to reduce claim costs. They will become more valuable in the years to come due to the predictions of increased medical costs and higher workers' comp claim activity. That makes nurse triage worth considering.

On average, for every dollar spent on nurse triage services, companies save $5-$10. Some nurse triage companies report that for every two calls they receive, one is referred to the appropriate medical provider, while the other is self-treated with medical oversight by the nurse, which saves a considerable amount, compared to charges by clinics or hospitals for care.

A sample of results reported by users of Nurse Triage services has reported the following:

1. Reduced workers' comp claims by 30%
2. Cut incurred costs by $1,600,000
3. Decreased lag time in injury reporting from 17 days to 2 days on average
4. Lawsuits down by almost 40%
5. Reduction in Emergency Room usage by 25%
6. Claims cost savings of up to 25-30%
7. Enhanced Return to Work results
8. Medical provider network usage improved to 98%.

Go to the appendix, page 219, for more details on nurse triage and how it can be another key to your profitability.

Nurse Case Management (NCM)

Nurse Case Management is another service to consider in your strategy for reducing workers' compensation costs. Similar to nurse triage services, nurse case management services help ensure that claim activities and medical treatments provided to the injured employee are facilitated in an expedient manner.

The worst thing that you can do in managing a workers' comp case is to blindly trust that everything will fall into place with regards to claim activity and medical treatment. Nurse case managers are trained professionals, typically Registered Nurses (RN) or Licensed Practical Nurses (LPN).

One of the main goals of a nurse case manager is to help facilitate your injured employee's return to work as quickly as possible. They can be very helpful in:

1. Arranging medical provider appointments
2. Making sure prescriptions are filled
3. Coordinating any diagnostic testing that needs to be done (CT Scan, EMG, MRI, etc.)
4. Arranging for durable medical equipment, if needed
5. Coordinating communication with insurance company adjusters
6. Ensuring injured employees understand the process

There are times when the insurance company at no additional cost to you can supply nurse case management. Depending upon your level of need, you may want to retain the services of outside nurse case management companies to help you reduce your workers' comp costs. Go to the appendix page 224, for more detailed information on what nurse case management is and how it is being utilized by companies today.

Six Very Important Words

At this point, we have discussed important documentation needed at the onset of any claim to help your adjuster keep your claim costs down.

Let me now share with you something that may be even more important. If you remember nothing else, please remember this. The six most important words in dealing with an injured employee are these: "Make Sure They Know You Care."

Seriously! Statistics show repeatedly, that an employee who doesn't feel you care is more likely to go out and find an attorney.

Relationships matter!

"Make Sure They Know You Care"

Even if you suspect an employee is trying to take advantage of you and the system, do yourself a favor by having a smile on your face and treating them with care and respect. There may be times when that will be a very hard pill to swallow, but trust me, if you kill your employees with kindness, they will be less apt to seek legal counsel.

I am not suggesting you buy a dozen roses and send a box of chocolates to their house following an accident, but I am suggesting you do whatever it takes to help them gain a sense that you care about them and want them back to work as soon as possible.

One of the best leading indicators in the success of your claim is the quality of the relationship between the injured employee and supervisor. The relationship the supervisors have with the staff they manage is huge. This cannot be overstated. The supervisor should play an active role in conveying their concern for the injured employee and their family, providing reassurance that they sincerely care.

Supervisor training

Have you trained your supervisors on their role in dealing with an injured employee after a claim? If not, put this on your "TO DO" list.

In the next chapter

I take a brief departure from discussions about workers' compensation and talk about another area that will impact your profitability as a company. I am referring to the subject of "Wellness." Many people are concerned about the impact and liabilities of the new Affordable Care Act (ACA) on their business. A wellness program, implemented properly, will help reduce the cost of your healthcare program, which will increase your profitability.

"You have got to say, I think that if I keep working at this and want it badly enough I can have it. It is called perseverance."

~ *Lee Iacocca*

Chapter 16:

Wellness

Most of my discussion so far has focused on the implementation of policies and procedures considered "best practices" in the administration of a sound workers' compensation program.

There is an absolute correlation between the effectiveness of a wellness program and its ability to reduce workers' compensation claims and their costs. If your employees are in poor physical condition due to obesity, smoking, or diabetes, their recovery time after an injury will be more difficult, take longer and add to the cost of your claim.

For the safety of the employee, doctors may need to wait months before performing needed surgery to repair a workers' comp injury. Sometimes, for example, a doctor may require the employee to lose weight before performing back surgery. Having to wait for needed care only adds to the overall cost of your claim.

In a report published by Duke University, their medical center analysis found obese workers filed twice the number of workers' compensation claims, had seven times higher medical costs for those claims and lost 13 times more days of work due to injury or work illness than their non-obese workers. (http://www.dukehealth.org/health_library/news/10044)

With some medical procedures, employees that smoke hamper their body's ability to heal quickly. Broken bones, for example, will not mend or fuse properly because of the effect of smoking on their body.

These days, because everyone is having to do more work with less people, it is critical your staff stay healthy and productive. Health has a major influence on productivity.

Whether an employee is injured at work, which triggers a workers' compensation claim, or falls ill and needs treatment, do your best to protect them from injury and keep them healthy. Doing so keeps your business running smoothly.

Encourage employee participation in health and wellness programs

At a time when health care costs and health insurance premiums continue to skyrocket, companies are looking for systems and methods that will produce better results than traditional wellness programs of the past. Today things have changed, and with new legislation on the books, companies can now implement programs to encourage more employee participation in their own health and wellness, which drives down insurance costs.

Because of the synergies between workers' compensation and health insurance, companies are partnering with firms that have systems capable of proficiently handling both platforms. The legal complexities of workers' comp and health insurance provide another good reason for companies to contract with firms that can coordinate both programs together. This makes sense, since it is critical to comply with a myriad of government regulations: FMLA, ADA, & COBRA, and many others. Many companies today are concerned for the liabilities and costs of the new Health Care System.

A quick note on Health Care Reform (HCR). Misinformation is rampant. Make sure you are receiving counsel from individuals who have credentials as a Certified Health Care Reform Specialist. Look for the following seal.

As you can imagine, there are times when HR issues blur. It may not be clear whether workers' compensation or health insurance will respond to your employee's accident or condition. How many times has an employee missed work and it wasn't clear how their condition started? Was it a workers' compensation injury or was it caused by conditions outside of work? Were they actively at work when the issue started? Do I file a claim under workers' comp so the employee does not incur a co-pay or deductible with their health insurance coverage?

Sometimes the answer isn't easy to sort out.

In recent years, employers have come to understand the importance of wellness, and many have worked to implement company-wide programs, but with limited success. They offered employees health screenings or gym memberships to promote wellness initiatives, but, because people are creatures of habit, only a few took advantage of the opportunity to improve their health.

Create wellness programs that motivate participation

Now recent legislation permits companies to create wellness programs that motivate people to participate. People are being motivated today by having "skin in the game," based on the idea that if you affect their pocketbook, employees will pay attention and take action on their own behalf.

Wellness programs today go beyond health screenings to determine possible health issues. Instead, they offer incentives for healthier behaviors. Health benchmarks are created at the beginning of any wellness program. The system rewards those who show improvement on these health indicators by reducing their health insurance premiums.

Employees who choose not to participate in your wellness program or who fail to improve their health-related conditions will pay higher premiums than their healthier counterparts.

You have heard the adage, "What Gets Measured Gets Done." This is never truer than when trying to drive better results with healthcare costs. Companies often saw less than 50% participation in their traditional wellness programs. Today, employees realize it will cost them money if they neglect their health. That's part of the reason today's wellness programs have participation rates of over 95%.

Establishing benchmarks

So, you might ask, what do we measure? Benchmarks are established by reviewing biometric levels in such areas as:

1. BMI (body mass index)
2. Blood sugar
3. Cholesterol
4. Smoking/non-Smoking
5. Weight

We all know at least one over-achiever in our company whom we envy because their body fat is fewer than 5% and can run a half-marathon without breaking a sweat. ☺ The system you set up takes into account that you have employees whose health conditions run from A – Z.

Effective wellness programs will take time to mature. Most companies begin with conservative benchmarks, and simply require employees to show improvement in overall health over a given period. Those whose health improved will pay less for their health insurance than they had previously paid. Employees with chronic health conditions can receive coaching and assistance to help them stay on track with their goals.

One company experienced 99% participation and realized a net savings of $124 per employee

In just three years, companies have experienced tremendous cost reductions with the new approach to employee wellness, and as a result, they've also increased profitability.

At one company, 99%+ employees participated in the wellness program. 7.6% stopped smoking, and 16.4% reduced their BMI factors two points or more, for net savings of $124 per employee per year. That success gave them good reason to continue to invest in wellness programs. Clearly, the savings from lower insurance costs and increased productivity far exceed the cost of a wellness program.

In the Appendix, page 229, you will find more success stories from companies that have implemented effective wellness programs. It is all about results. When your wellness program is deployed properly, you will experience higher productivity, fewer workers' compensation claims, and lower health care costs.

"Even if you are on the right track,

you'll get run over if you just sit there."

~ Will Rogers

Chapter 17:

An insurance carrier's perspective...

From an insurance carrier perspective, one of our primary goals is to control claims costs. We seek policyholders that follow "Best Practices" guidelines, as suggested in this book. Below is a list of programs and policies by the types of companies that we would like to insure.

1. **Safety:** One of the most effective and successful ways to avoid workers' compensation claims and provide your employees with a safe working environment is to implement and monitor a formal safety program. An effective safety program should be strategically designed, based on the individual exposures of each insured.

2. **Pre-Employment and Hiring**: In order to hire the right people for the position, appropriate testing and evaluation is imperative before the position is offered.

3. **Train Supervisors and Managers**: Awareness, consistency and participation in management directives are necessary for positive results.

4. **Educate Employees About Their Rights and Responsibilities**: This could reduce litigation and

improve employee satisfaction with the handling of their claims.

5. **Report Claims Promptly**: Early notification allows for thorough investigation, timely delivery of benefits, better management and reduced litigation.

6. **Thorough Investigation**: This process may identify fraud and ultimately reduce claims costs. Additionally, it allows for the development of rapport with employees.

7. **Return to Work Program**: A Return to Work program has the potential to reduce dramatically the cost of any lost-time claim, and is a critical component to a successful policyholder.

8. **Medical Management**: Look for carriers that provide 3-point contact within 24 hours of a claim notification. Contact will be made with the injured employee, the employer and the medical facility. Securing the details early in a claims investigation is another step toward successful resolution of a claim.

9. **Risk Management**: A written, detailed program reduces the cost to the insured by reduced claims activity and a lower experience modification factor. In many states, schedule credits can be applied to those policyholders that have a Risk Management program.

10. **Safety Education**: Teach your employees to identify exposures that will prevent claims.

An insurance underwriter receives many applications each day. Those potential policyholders that follow the above practices will be given priority handling. We look for ways to be creative and underwrite businesses that demonstrate a desire to reduce losses.

To get the most favorable review of your application, it is crucial that your company adhere to the practices listed above, as well as follow the recommendations in Rick's book. In conclusion, we will be aggressive in our efforts to be the carrier of choice for those accounts where Best Practices are the standard and management is proactive in holding down the cost of claims.

Questions? You can reach Eleanor Powell-Yoder at (941)921-0629 or through the company's website: www.mcim.com

Eleanor Powell-Yoder, President, CEO

Michigan Commercial Insurance Mutual (MCIM)

"Most of the important things in the world have been accompanied by people who have kept on trying when there seemed to be no hope at all."

~Dale Carnegie

Chapter 18:

Attorneys Weigh in on the Issues

Have you ever second-guessed yourself, wondering if your handling of a business situation was going to get you into legal trouble, even if you felt you were doing everything right?

It happens every day with the best of companies. They find themselves being tapped on the shoulder with an employee lawsuit. Not only is this a frustrating event and a process to endure, but also a very costly one to your company's bottom line. I thought it would be helpful for you to get the perspective of two attorneys who specialize in the relevant areas of law to help you avoid a potential employee lawsuit.

Attorney James Kidd, senior partner at the law firm of Moran and Kidd, specializes in workers' compensation law and defends employers on workers' compensation issues. Attorney Keith Hammond is a partner at the law firm of Jackson Lewis LLP, a nationally known law firm specializing in employment law.

I sat down with them both and asked them a series of questions that employers across the country have asked me during my seminars. The following pages include new insights, and endorse many of the principles we have examined together thus far.

Interview with Attorney James Kidd, Workers' Compensation Law Specialist

Rick Dalrymple: (RD) **James, if there were five top business practices companies should be mindful of to avoid lawsuits, what would they be?**

James Kidd: (JK) First, I recommend they look at their pre-hiring and post-hiring practices. Screening perspective employees is critical in making sure that you have individuals who will be good for your organization. During the pre-employment process, clarify any gaps in their employment history. You also want to see stability in their employment history, and that they provide your organization with the information needed to assess them as a candidate.

During the post-hiring process, verify they have completed all the necessary forms. Once hired, educate new employees about your organization. Let them know what your organization expects concerning safety, the reporting of accidents, testing procedures and processes. Your company's pre and post-hire process is step number one.

Number two is to implement a strong safety program. This not only means having a safety manager in place, but also making a commitment to a culture of safety that comes from the top of your organization. Make sure safety is a part of the education process, and part of the day-to-day work environment for your company. Companies that have a commitment to safety and a strong safety program are going to be more successful in avoiding accidents, reducing the severity of accidents, and ultimately limiting litigation.

Step Three involves having a strong 'accident reporting' and 'provision of care' procedure in place. Once an accident does occur, timely investigation and proper reporting to your carrier are crucial. Also, verify that the injured worker is sent to the appropriate providers for immediate treatment. You want to make sure their injury can be diagnosed, and that the injured worker can be provided the necessary treatment for a speedy recovery.

JK: Having these procedures in place allows you to properly investigate the accident and to make sure that it's consistent as initially reported. You only want to deal with and provide treatment for conditions and injuries which are work related.

JK: Step Four is a successful Return to Work
program. I know IOA Risk Services is a strong
proponent of Return to Work programs and
actively assist their clients with developing
such programs. In my experience, my
employers and clients with a commitment to a
Return to Work program mitigate their
exposure and the severity of their claims. I
cannot over emphasize the importance of a
strong Return to Work program.

Step Five involves having your defense team
in place. If you want to mitigate your exposure
in litigation, you need a strong defense team,
which starts with the employer's
representative in charge of the claims within
the company. It could be a safety director, a
risk manager, or a human resource
representative. Regardless of their position,
designate one individual to communicate with
your carrier or servicing agent. Next, if
possible, have a dedicated adjuster for your
account, who handles all of your claims. This
allows the adjuster to become familiar with
your organization. They should work in unison
with your employer representative and make
sure the proper medical providers get
involved, and that the employee returns to
work as soon as possible. Finally, for cases
that go into litigation, make sure your

RD: **James how would you counsel your clients on the best way to handle perceived fraud cases?**

JK: First, I think clients need to understand what the fraud statute is and the standard under their state's workers' compensation law. You hear a lot of employers or individuals referencing fraud, and while there are certainly cases of employees malingering and exaggerating symptoms, these activities do not necessarily rise to the level of misrepresentation under workers' compensation law. So, any time I have an employer concerned about possible fraud, the first step is to explain the legal standard of what fraud is. In Florida, workers' compensation fraud involves an employee knowingly and intentionally providing false, fraudulent or misleading information for the purposes of securing workers' compensation benefits.

RD: **Is that hard to prove?**

JK: The 'intent' element is the difficult part to prove, and you certainly want to have evidence that supports or shows intent, such as documentation of a prior injury or an inaccurate history provided to a doctor. Often you need the doctor to provide strong testimony that the individual gave them an inaccurate or inconsistent history based on prior or pre-existing medical records. It's best to have multiple instances where the individual provided false or misleading information. The number of occasions and timing of the individual providing false information clearly helps establish the intent element necessary for a judge to find the individual in violation of state statutes.

RD: **James, in your experience, what types of red flag indicators should employers be mindful of as it relates to fraud?**

JK: One of the most prevalent indicators is the timing of the accident. You often see the Monday morning accident, the accident that occurs within the first week of hire, or un-witnessed accidents. You'll see accidents reported shortly before a project is coming to an end, or prior to a layoff. You often see an accident reported following disciplinary actions against individuals or when an employee fears termination. In any of those situations, you should be mindful of the potential for a false claim.

RD: **What should an employer do if they suspect fraud from one of their employees?**

JK: I'm a big believer in the method and process of claims handling. You need to be consistent. Make sure the steps you take from completing the initial accident report, obtaining witness statements and timely reporting to your carrier are done on every claim. So even if you perceive potential fraud, your method and claim handling process should not change. However, your concerns regarding the validity of the claim should be clearly documented and communicated to your carrier, assigned adjuster, and investigator. This should occur when first reporting the claim. This information and these concerns should assist and shape their investigation.

RD: **How does an employer position themselves properly to terminate a poor performing employee who has filed a workers' comp claim?**

JK: Under the current workers' compensation law, there is no obligation for an employer to rehire or make work available to an injured employee. However, Return to Work programs are important and encouraged. They mitigate your exposure. Most employers are going to have an employee back to work post-accident. In Florida, for example, the retaliation section of the Statute 440.205 prohibits employers from any adverse action against an employee who has filed or reported a workers' compensation claim. If adverse action is taken, employees may bring a Circuit Court cause of action seeking relief. When dealing with employment issues with an individual who has a workers' compensation claim, I advise my client to not change or deviate from their standard employment practices. Instead, it is critical to follow your company policies and procedures for documenting any violations, written warnings, and disciplinary actions. Your enforcement should be the same as it has for other employees who do not have any claims.

RD: **So if an employee is suspected of taking advantage of the system, the employer is free to terminate on the basis of their performance, as long as the poor performance has been properly documented.**

JK: Yes, employers need to make sure they handle the documentation the same way they document other employees' performance. Issue warnings and reprimands for poor performance just as you would to any employee found violating company performance policies.

Say, for example, you write up an employee for being tardy at work and you have issued three warnings for tardiness. If company policy says the fourth tardy shall result in termination, and you routinely enforce that policy, you can do so with an individual who has a pending workers' compensation claim. However, if other employees regularly show up late, and you fail to write them up, you're not enforcing that policy consistently for being tardy. By not enforcing that policy with all your employees, you're going to get into problems. If you enforce company policies the same way with all employees, you should be fine. I also strongly recommend you always consult legal counsel to review the file for sufficiency of documentation and adequacy of grounds for termination before terminating an employee.

RD: **James, you're familiar with the salary-in-lieu-of-comp strategy that some employers use? They elect to pay the employee's wages rather than the carrier. How comfortable are you when employers take this step in order to reduce the cost of their claim?**

JK: I am familiar with this practice, and I'm very comfortable with it. In some cases, it can be an effective tool. It is not a strategy that can be utilized in every case. It should be considered on a case-by-case basis if your employment policies permit this practice. Key issues are the length of expected disability and your ability to return the individual to work in a modified position as quickly as possible. Certainly if you're able to avoid a lost time claim by paying salary for a brief period in lieu of workers' compensation benefits, it's going to have a positive impact on your insurance costs.

RD: **Do you feel the medical community contributes to abuses in the workers' comp system?**

JK: Anyone familiar with workers' compensation realizes that medical treatment and medical costs are a huge component of overall claim costs. Thus, I encourage employers to be aware of the impact of medical costs on their claims. I recommend, when possible, they develop relationships with primary care physicians and other doctors, and help them become familiar with your company. Routinely send individuals to these providers for treatment, make doctors aware of your Return to Work program, and assist them in getting injured workers' back on the job, which is consistent with the intent outlined in the statutes. Finally, it is important to note if you lose medical control of your files, you're going to have more severe claims. In my opinion, one of the most significant problems is medication use. That's something we all need to be aware of, and it's certainly not limited to workers' compensation claims.

RD: **As a workers' comp attorney that represents employers, what do you think contributes most to employees seeking legal**

counsel for their workers' compensation claims?

JK:

A lot of factors may drive an individual to seek counsel, but some you see much more frequently than others. One, for lack of a better description, is the forgotten employee who is injured and feels forgotten by their employer. They feel "kicked to the curb." Employers, post-accident, need to let employees know you care. Employers who help shepherd them through the process are more likely to prevent some individuals from seeking legal counsel. A second cause is the failure to timely provide medical care. People have different pain thresholds and different reactions. An injured employee who feels they're not being properly cared for is going to seek legal counsel. You want to make sure they receive prompt medical attention. From reporting the accident, to the carrier's authorization of care, any delay in medical care will drive people to attorneys.

Another common cause of conflict is poor communication when an employee returns to work in modified duty. Clear communication between management and front line supervisors is essential when an injured worker returns to work. You want to verify all assigned work is within the prescribed restrictions. Often supervisors are worried about productivity, meeting quotas, getting the job done, and they fail to abide by the employee's work restrictions. They fail to show a willingness to work with the injured employee and this drives the employees to seek legal representation. The commitment to work restrictions needs to come from the top. Failing to follow restrictions set by the physician often triggers the hiring of an attorney. The failure to have a Return to Work program in place can also contribute. Have you ever watched TV during the work day? You're bombarded with commercials about hiring an attorney. If your employees are working and feeling like they're getting back into the swing of things, they are less likely to see those TV commercials and go and seek out counsel.

RD: **In the future, do you see workers' compensation lawsuits increasing or decreasing in their number and size?**

JK: I expect to see an increase in workers' compensation claims, especially in certain industries. The economy has been tough over the past several years. The tight job market has discouraged many employees from reporting and pursuing workers' compensation claims because they value their job. As the economy turns around, especially in certain industries where employees feel like they can readily change employers, I expect to see an increase in the number of claims. I don't have any basis to indicate that claims are going to become more severe and more costly. While pharmaceutical costs and medical expenses have increased, wages have remained fairly flat. Thus, I haven't seen an increase in the severity of claims from an indemnity standpoint, as much as from the medical perspective.

RD: **Do you feel that most Workers' Comp lawsuits are avoidable?**

JK: In a large number of cases, the key to avoiding workers' comp claims and lawsuits is to avoid the injury and incident itself. Often that's going to come down to proper safety, policies and procedures, training and education of your workforce, proper supervision and a safe work culture. Once the incidents or the accidents have occurred and are reported, you must take steps to avoid a lawsuit. We have touched on that already, but it gets back to a phrase that I've heard you use a hundred times: "kill 'em with kindness." Make sure you give employees the attention they need, educate them on the workers' comp process, make sure they get proper treatment, and get their claim in the hands of your carrier or servicing agent for processing. Do it right, and you're likely to face fewer obstacles.

RD: **James, do you have any interesting cases that employers can learn from?**

JK: I recently had a case involving numerous claims including a request for lost wages, ongoing care, and permanent total disability benefits. In preparing our defense for this trial, I had the full cooperation of the employer and carrier. This claim demonstrates the importance of having patience and trusting your claims handling procedures.

This individual injured her low back in April 2009, and the accident and claim were accepted as compensable. The employer had a successful Return to Work program and following the accident provided the employee with modified duty work. She retained counsel, and initially filed a claim for permanent total disability benefits in March of 2011.

Despite this claim, the company continued to provide modified duty work. We established through the evidence and testimony of our vocational experts that this work was appropriate and within the individual's restrictions. The employer provided her modified duty for 26 months post-accident. When she violated the company's attendance policy, disciplinary protocols were followed. Once she exceeded her allowable points, she was terminated. The company hired a replacement for the position, which enabled us to establish the job would have remained available for the Claimant had she not been terminated for cause.

Early in this claim, we had received evidence that this individual did have some prior back problems; nothing significant, but clearly she had not been completely forthright with the medical providers, the employer, and the carrier. At that point, we could have asserted a misrepresentative defense under FS 440.105. However, the Employer/Carrier made a smart decision. They realized that while the injured worker hadn't been completely honest, this evidence wasn't strong enough to support a 440.105 misrepresentation defense. Thus, we continued to work and establish our other defenses.

Through the litigation process, we determined she had a subsequent motor vehicle accident in December 2011. As a result of that accident, she began receiving medical treatments. She did not advise the employer or carrier of this accident. In addition, a new petition requesting ongoing care for her accident was filed.

The adjuster timely and properly authorized a return visit to her provider. Next, we verified that the provider had the complete medical records from her intervening motor vehicle accident, for his review and consideration. The physician questioned her in detail concerning any accidents and injuries that she had been involved in or treatment she had received in the interim. She denied any new accidents, injuries, or other treatments. However, given the amount of medical evidence available and the timing of her treatment, we determined we had extremely strong evidence of misrepresentation.

Once we obtained the evidence through medical records and from the doctor's testimony, we asserted the 440.105 defense. We went to trial and prevailed not only on our "permanent total disability" defense based on the employer's Return to Work program, but also on the misrepresentation defense. The judge entered an order completely barring this individual from receiving any future treatment or benefits under this claim. This is an example of employer and carrier doing all the right things: being patient working their claim, commitment to their Return to Work program, and working as a team.

As a bonus to our readers, James is available for a 30-minute consultation to discuss your workers' compensation defense handling procedures and practices at no charge.

Attorney James Kidd
jfkidd@morankidd.com
www.morankidd.com
407-841-4141

Interview with Attorney Keith Hammond, Employment Law Specialist

Rick Dalrymple (RD): I'm here with Keith Hammond, a partner at Jackson Lewis, who specializes in labor law. I thought we'd go over some labor law questions related to workers' comp. **As a labor law and employment law attorney representing employers, what do you think motivates most employees to seek legal counsel on their workers comp claim?**

Keith Hammond (KH): Employees seek legal counsel for a number of reasons. Probably the main reason is the employees perception that he or she is not being treated fairly. A common question employees ask an attorney is: can my company require me to do this? Although many times the answer is "yes," the attorney may discover something else that's not right. For example, the attorney might discover a potential wage and hour violation when the employee originally sought their help for reasons wholly unrelated to compensation.

RD: **In labor and employment law, there is something called the "Bermuda Triangle", which refers to the interplay between the laws governing workers' comp, FMLA and ADA. What do employers need to be aware of to avoid this issue?**

KH: The Bermuda Triangle occurs when an employee is injured on the job badly enough to constitute a serious health condition as defined by the FMLA, and also as a disability as defined by the Americans with Disabilities Act (ADA). ADA, FMLA and the workers' comp laws have some "areas of discord," where the laws don't always jibe. One example that relates to those areas would be with respect to a supervisor's ability to contact and employee's health provider. Under the workers' comp law in Florida, the supervisor is permitted to reach out directly to the health provider. However, under the FMLA, a supervisor cannot do so. Those differences can land you in the Bermuda Triangle about whether it's appropriate for the supervisor to contact the health provider directly.

Generally the answer is no.

Under the FMLA, a head of HR or a non-direct supervisor, somebody further up the chain or not supervising the employee directly can contact the health provider for a limited number of reasons, such as to clarify an ambiguity on a certification form, *but only with the consent of the employee*. The ADA also permits contact with a physician in certain limited circumstances. For example, to evaluate an employee's ability to perform a job with or without a reasonable accommodation. The triangle refers to areas of incongruence where one law permits certain employer actions, which one or both of the other laws prohibit.

RD: **How do you avoid stepping in a bucket by doing the wrong thing?**

KH: [laughing] Obviously, having written policies and procedures in place that comply with the law is the first step. Your next step is to actually comply with your policies and procedures. It's generally not the head of HR who gets the company in trouble. Typically, it's lower-level supervisors who tend to overstep their bounds and do something inappropriate - usually because they didn't know the law or didn't really know company policy.

RD: **How do you deal with an employee who is capable of coming back to work after a workers' comp injury, but whose work quality deteriorates? Can you terminate the employee while reducing and/or eliminating the risk of a retaliation lawsuit?**

KH: Risk will never be zero. But certainly there are steps you can take to minimize your company's risk. Communication is the first step. Use effective communication with employees, telling them what the deficiency is, and why it's important they correct it. Documentation comes next. Document, document, document. One of the first questions an employer will be asked in an unemployment comp proceeding or a lawsuit is: did you tell the employee what he or she was doing wrong? Naturally, you want to avoid giving the impression that you're just papering the file to set them up for termination. If, however, you have a progressive discipline policy, such as: verbal warning for the first violation, written warning for the second and suspension or termination after the third time an employee commits the same infraction - that goes a long way, both in the unemployment comp arena and in front of a jury. It all supports the contention that the employer is being fair and evenhanded with the employee, and consistent in the use of proper procedures to correct the problematic behavior.

RD: **Why is it such a challenge to comply with FMLA, ADA and workers' comp?**

KH: Knowing the law is Step One; keeping up with it is Step Two. All of these laws are changing constantly. But another challenge I've observed is communication with an employee on leave can be difficult. The employee is not in the office every day. As a supervisor, you may not have the chance to speak directly with the employee. Many times supervisors don't bother to place a phone call to the employee just to see how things are going or to note that FMLA leave will expire in a week. Sometimes it's the fault of the employee who doesn't return a phone call, but overall the communication issue, I think, is one of the things that make dealing with these leave laws so challenging.

RD: **Could you briefly describe the purpose of each of these laws, and explain how they generate such confusion?**

KH: Sure. Each of these laws was enacted for different purposes, which are sometimes in conflict. The FMLA was enacted to allow employees to balance work commitments and family life. For example, it provides for reasonable unpaid leave for a variety of circumstances ranging from caring for your own or a family member's serious health condition to military exigency. The ADA was not designed primarily as a leave law. Instead, it affords employment opportunities to qualified persons with disabilities who historically had been bypassed for jobs that they were perfectly capable of performing. Finally, the workers' comp law was enacted to reduce workplace litigation. The tradeoff with the workers' comp statute is that the employee injured on the job receives certain benefits, and employers don't have to litigate every slip and fall in the workplace, which would be far more expensive than just paying out benefits under the workers' comp statute.

RD: **How do you determine which law applies?**

KH: You need to evaluate each law on its own. The workers' comp law will apply if an employee is injured on the job as a result of some form of negligence or conduct that's less than gross negligence. The FMLA applies if you're a certain size employer and if the employee is taking or requesting leave for one of the reasons specifically articulated in the statute. Finally the ADA requires an evaluation as to whether the employee has a mental or physical condition that substantially limits a major life activity. In some instances, all three laws might apply. For example if the employee suffers an on-the-job injury that results in a serious health condition under the FMLA that's also a disability under ADA, then all three laws apply. In other instances, though, only one or two of the three might apply, which makes it slightly easier for the employer. Nonetheless it's important to know all three laws.

RD: **And the number of employees for FMLA is what, over 50?**

KH: That's correct. FMLA also requires that the individual be an eligible employee. That is, he or she must have worked for the company (with 50 or more employees) 12 months or more, worked at least 1,250 hours during the preceding year, and worked at a worksite within 75 miles of the company's location. So let's say an employer has 500 employees. It is easily covered by the FMLA, but the employee requesting leave is stationed at an outpost hundreds of miles away from the next closest employee. That employee might not be eligible for FMLA leave.

RD: **What policies and procedures are the most critical to have in place to avoid employee lawsuits?**

KH: Of course your policies must comply with the law. If you're covered by FMLA, the law requires you to have an FMLA policy and to post an FMLA notice to your employees. Likewise, it's important to have a policy that you, as an employer, will afford a reasonable accommodation to a qualified individual with a disability. More important than the written policies and procedures though, in my opinion, is that supervisors and managers know the policies and comply with them. So to that end, training is equally as important as having the policies in the first place.

RD: **What are your recommendations for auditing policies and procedures?**

KH: It's a good idea to have an employment lawyer review your employee handbook every year or so. New cases come out all the time addressing the FMLA or the ADA. In fact, within the last couple of years, both those laws have seen changes to their regulations, if not, to the statutes themselves. So we're dealing with areas of the law that are in constant flux and although your policy may have been compliant in 2008, it may not be compliant in 2013.

RD: **Have you noticed any trend toward increases in the number of employee lawsuits in the future and, if so, what areas of law seem most problematic?**

KH: That's an interesting question – one might think that the answer is, "yes," that the number of suits goes up every year in a linear pattern, and that's not entirely true. From 1997 to 2007, for example, the number of EEOC charges filed nationwide fluctuated between 75,000 and 85,000, and the number went up and down over the course of those 11 years. Over the last three years, however, we've seen an explosion in EEOC filings which rose by almost 100,000 per year, which is an approximate 20% increase from 2007. We've also seen a number of lawsuits being brought under the Fair Labor Standards Act, which doesn't have a lot to do with workers' comp, but it may worth noting. Here in Florida, in the mid-2000s, we saw an explosion of wage and hour litigation that hasn't receded yet, and in other parts of the country we're seeing the same trend.

RD: **Why do you think there has been an explosion of lawsuits in the last several years?**

KH: It could be a combination of things; the economy certainly is one reason. Many people lost jobs over the last three to four years, and losing a job is one of those triggering events that could lead to a lawsuit.

I think that the proliferation of attorneys handling employment law matters on behalf of employees could be a reason as well. I think there are more attorneys in the marketplace and more advertising. It's easy to find an attorney who will answer an employment law question these days, whereas 10, 15, 20 years ago that may not have been the case.

RD: **What is your recommendation for an employer who, let's say, reassigns an employee for return to work purposes, but the employee does not really want to accept that reassignment.**

KH: Well, this is one of the areas of the Bermuda Triangle that requires careful navigation. Under the FMLA, an employee has the right to reject a light duty job or any job that's not identical or substantially similar to the position that he or she left when the period of leave began. For workers' comp, however, an employer may want to offer light duty and, if the employee rejects it, the employee's indemnity benefits might be cut off. Finally, under the ADA, you may be required to place an employee into a vacant position. You don't have to create a position under the ADA, but if a position within the employee's abilities is vacant, the act may require you to place the employee in that position as a reasonable accommodation.

RD: **If you could provide, 10 tips for managing the interplay between ADA, FMLA and workers' comp, what would they be? For example, you hear people talking about knowing your leave policies and training supervisors and human resource compliance, what do you say?**

KH: Rick, you really hit the nail right on the head. Certainly, knowing the leave policies and training your supervisors are critical. Having a trained human resources staff that can manage difficult situations is important if you're a large enough employer. If you have in-house legal counsel, there are likely to be instances where you want to confer with them. If not, you might confer with external counsel. Remember that under each of these laws, a proposed accommodation or offer to return to work has to be evaluated on a case-by-case basis. At the same time, you've got to maintain consistency in your decision making. You don't want to treat an employee on leave any differently than you treat similarly situated employees. And avoid overstepping your bounds in requesting medical documentation. If you do have properly obtained medical documentation, use it to be sure that you're not setting your employee up to fail by offering a position beyond his or her limitations.

KH: But here's the bottom line, Rick. Communication is the key: both communication with the employee and internal communication within your company. Effective communication between the HR department, the supervisor, and in some cases, the workers' comp adjuster, is critical.

RD: **Do you have any interesting cases that employers could learn from?**

KH: Well, I can tell you this with respect to all cases that I see as opposed to a one-off case where there were some specialized facts. If you're an employer finding yourself in litigation, you will see the following. The employee's lawyer will ask what type of training the company conducts for supervisors so they know how to comply with the law. You know you will be asked for copies of your policies. If the EEOC is investigating a charge of discrimination, they will likely want to see your employee handbook or, at a minimum, your EEO policies or leave policies. The current trend is for the EEOC to examine whether an employer's leave policy requires automatic termination of an employee unable to return at the end of FMLA leave. That could violate the ADA. Let's say an employee only needs another week of unpaid leave to be able to come back to work, the EEOC could find that a reasonable accommodation would be to allow the employee another week of leave. So having this automatic termination policy could run afoul of the ADA. Similarly, if the Department of Labor (DOL) investigates your company, the first thing it will ask to see will be your posters. They are looking for is not only a wage and hour poster, but also for your FMLA poster. If you don't have that poster displayed in a conspicuous area, at best the DOL will give you the poster to hang up. At worst, they might find an FMLA violation.

RD: **How does an employer position itself to properly terminate a poor performing employee who has filed a workers' compensation claim?**

KH: An employee should never be surprised by a termination. They should receive fair notice that their performance is not up to snuff, and they should be given the opportunity to correct it. In that regard, an employee who's filed the workers' comp claim is no different from a worker who has not. Of course, with the workers' comp employee; you run the risk that the termination could be perceived as retaliation for going out on workers' comp leave in the first place. And while there's no way to eliminate the risk, you can certainly minimize it through good communication, through a progressive discipline policy, and by giving the employee the opportunity to cure whatever deficiency he or she is exhibiting.

RD: **What mistakes do you most often see employers make that creates unnecessary lawsuits?**

KH: I would say there are two categories here. One would be employers who simply don't know the law. While I find them to be somewhat few and far between, they're out there. The other main category would be conduct that, while perfectly legal on the part of the employer, leaves a bad taste in the mouth of the employee. In other words, the employee perceives he or she is not being treated fairly. That's what drives employees to talk to lawyers. Now, nobody's perfect. Everybody makes mistakes. But, the employee who feels set up to fail, is more likely to be disgruntled and go see an attorney. The company then winds up with a lawsuit on its hands.

RD:

What are the key elements of the hiring process employers need to be mindful of to avoid a discrimination lawsuit?

KH:

In hiring, it's important for employers to be mindful that they are looking for the best-suited candidate for the job, and unfortunately, employers sometimes consider factors that have nothing to do with job performance. For example, if an employee comes into an interview in a wheelchair and the job is a desk job, there's no need to ask if they can perform the essential functions with or without a reasonable accommodation. That's a permissible question, but if the condition isn't one that would impact their ability to do the job, why ask that question? And of course, you know there's no need to have other information about protected classes such as age, race, etc., when making a hiring decision. Granted, you obtain that information post hire, but pre-hire, there's really no need to seek it beforehand.

RD:

Do you advocate employers having applicants complete a medical questionnaire after they've offered a job? Some HR professionals suggest it's better *not* to know. What are your thoughts on that as it relates to having to make reasonable accommodations and getting questionnaires completed?

KH:

Again, there are two schools of thought, Rick. In one view, a post-offer medical questionnaire is a good tool for employers, primarily for workers' comp purposes. If an employee fails to disclose a past medical condition and then makes a workers' comp claim basically for the same condition, the carrier could deny the claim on the basis that the injury wasn't the result of a workplace accident or wasn't caused by or exacerbated by anything in the workplace. The other school of thought, though, maintains that it's better not to know if an employee has a medical history. I suspect they rely on the rationale that if you don't know, they can't be accused of discrimination. In many cases, however, the employee will self-disclose a condition post hire, triggering the requirement to engage in the interactive process to ascertain whether a reasonable accommodation is necessary or not. One note about medical questionnaires. One law we haven't yet discussed is called GINA, the Genetic Information Non-Disclosure Act, which prohibits an employer from asking about certain information: the genetic history of the applicant or the applicant's family, for example. So while it would be okay on a medical questionnaire to ask whether an employee has ever torn a rotator cuff or broken a bone, it would *not* be okay to ask if the applicant or the applicant's family has a history of cancer or diabetes.

RD: **If we were tipping the scales as to whether employers should use medical questionnaires, how do advise clients on this issue?**

KH: Provided that the questionnaire isn't asking for information in a fashion that would violate GINA, I'm okay with the caveat that it absolutely must be post-offer, not pre-offer. An employer should never ask an applicant, pre-offer, about his or her medical history.

RD: **You have done a remarkable job in mapping out these issues for employers. In closing, can you suggest a short list of the most important types of policies and procedures that companies need to have in place, to have audited, and to make sure the paperwork is in file.**

KH: First, if you are covered by the FMLA, meaning you have 50 or more employees, you must have an FMLA policy and you must post a notice of employees' rights under the FMLA.

RD: Okay.

KH: Regardless of your size, you should also have an EEO policy, an equal employment opportunity policy that prohibits discrimination on the basis of disability or any other protected class, such as race, color, religion, national origin, sex, or age. Most employers are covered by these EEO laws, even if they're not large enough to be covered by the FMLA. The threshold for Title VII, for example, is 15 employees. Even if you have fewer than 15 employees, your local ordinance or state law might have a lower threshold to clear. In addition to those two policies, I recommend having an accommodation policy.

In other words, a policy that says: If you are a qualified individual with a disability, and you require an accommodation to perform the essential functions of your job, please speak with HR or another designated person.

Your accommodation policy should explain that the accommodations will be considered on a case-by-case basis. You should not delineate a fine line between what the company will do or will not do to accommodate, because that indicates an evaluation is not being made case-by-case. I also recommend having a complaint procedure in place, so if an employee feels he or she has been discriminated against, has not been permitted to utilize FMLA leave, or has not been accommodated appropriately, he or she has an avenue to seek recourse. Additionally, I recommend having a written anti-retaliation policy to assure employees they won't be retaliated against for utilizing the complaint procedure. It's also important to have a progressive discipline policy in place, and this goes back to the fairness issues that we've been discussing. If an employee is terminated out of the blue, he or she is more likely to see an attorney than if he or she had been given ample warning of performance deficiencies. Finally, I advocate routine training for supervisors. The law is a difficult sea to navigate. It's difficult for lawyers, it's difficult for HR directors, yet the supervisors are generally the ones on the front lines, you know. They need to be well-trained in how to react to a particular situation.

If you have any questions regarding the issues discussed above or other workplace laws, you may schedule a complimentary initial consultation with Mr. Hammond by contacting him at (407) 246-8440.

Attorney Keith Hammond
HammondK@JacksonLewis.com
www.jacksonlewis.com

"Events in life have no meaning, other than the ones we give them....we choose to create empowering interpretations or negative interpretations. It is always our choice."

~Anonymous

Chapter 19:

Your Next Step

Before you read another line, **STOP** and register your book at www.RichardDalrymple.com. There you will have access to some of the vital resources and tools available to my clients and readers.

This final chapter will be rather short and to the point.

Your next step will determine your level of success in increasing your profitability as a company, that is, whether you and your business will be winners in this new economy.

As I see it, you have just three options.

OPTION #1. You can refuse to do anything. But expect the coming years to be hard on you and your company. Your time left is limited. But if you have gotten this far, I seriously doubt you will choose this fatal option.

OPTION #2. Using this book as your map, you can attempt to begin the process alone. Your company's future is at stake.

Using the information provided in prior chapters, you can create your own success story, and as a team leader, manage your success to the top. How? The path is clear:

- Research and assemble the policies and procedures referenced in this book.

- Reach out and hire professionals whose expertise you will need for various tasks.

- If possible, identify and hire a mentor from among these experts.

- Create a timeline with the appropriate milestones en route to attaining your goals.

- Work with your expert guides to implement the strategies and tactics in this book.

- Identify and secure the proper tools to accomplish your goals faster and more easily.

- Celebrate your success upon reaching each goal.

- After reaching your goals, review your milestones to ensure your new business model and systems are functioning properly; and, finally,

- Celebrate like hell for reaching your goals and contact me with the news. Congratulations will be in order!

There is a lot of work to do but the reward of increased profitability will be well worth the effort.

OPTION #3. As you embark on your journey to better profitability, I hope you discover that I have given you a fantastic start by providing a trustworthy map to direct you on your way.

Remember the lengthy "TO DO" list in option # 2?

It will take time, energy and persistence to organize and implement all of them into your organization. Although possible, it can be a daunting task to create an effective and easy-to-use workers' compensation administration system on your own.

So, you may be thinking right now, "I want help!" In the introduction, I promised to show you how to make your goals happen faster and more easily.

Being experts in the field, we have created a turnkey system that saves you time and cuts to the chase.

Our tools will streamline your workers' comp system for you. All you need to do is join our team at IOA Risk Services to help you reach your goals.

You can expect:

RESULTS... in better hiring procedures that reduce your employee turnover by over 30%, your number of claims by over 60% and the severity of those claims by over 21%.

RESULTS... in accessing compliance ready, profit-enhancing procedures that save you time and money.

RESULTS... in avoiding employee lawsuits.

RESULTS... in organizing your claim activity, enabling you to close claims faster and for less money, preventing lost corporate profits.

RESULTS... in streamlining and lowering your training costs and accessing easily identifiable trend reports.

RESULTS... in quickly determining your company's strengths, pinpointing areas for improvement, and achieving "Best Practices" status in workers' comp administration, saving your company hundreds of thousands of dollars in lost profits.

If you want to find out more about the our process, and how it can reduce your company's risk, lower your operating costs, and protect your profitability, start by getting your company's *RiskScore®*, at: www.WhatsMyRiskScore.com and fill out a brief interest form. It takes just a moment, and opens the door to your success and resources, quickly.

If you have questions, call me at (321) 578-7559 between 7:00 a.m. and 6:00 p.m. EST.

Congratulations!

Let me be the first to commend you for taking time to read this book. We have covered a lot of territory together, and it is my sincerest hope that you have found the material informative and insightful. I presume you have a lengthy "TO DO" list that you have updated while reading this book.

As I wrote in Chapter 1, it's one thing to have a workers' compensation policy in place. Even more important, what goals have you written down to improve your workers' compensation "system?"

Remember, there are only three options open to any company.

Whatever you choose, I wish you the best of luck in your journey. I want to hear from you soon, to find out how you are doing.

***

Don't stop here!

Please continue read and review the appendix which contains detailed information on the material outlined in this book.

Section III

APPENDIX

APPENDIX - CONTENTS

Behavioral Based Safety Systems

(Modern Safety Management)

Introduction

Since the industrial revolution traditional "safety programs" focused on hazard controls and employee training to prevent incidents. For over 100 years, these programs reduced the number and severity of workplace accidents, but they rarely produced incident free workplaces. In recent years, progressive organizations have achieved remarkable results by approaching safety management in a completely new way.

The Safety Evolution

Before we explore the modern safety management approach, it is important to see how workplace safety has evolved.

Stage 1

During the early 1900s, incidents were viewed as being caused by "faulty" workers. On average, there were 61 deaths per 100,000 workers. Societal pressure mounted for companies to improve dangerous working conditions. The earliest safety practitioner's "tool kit" consisted of incident reports, inspections and general awareness programs.

Stage 2

Around the Second World War, the focus shifted away from workers and on to dangerous machinery. Equipment was designed with safeguards to help prevent injuries. The safety tool kit expanded to include training, orientations, investigations, and supervisor development. During this stage, fatality rates fell to 37 deaths per 100,000 workers.

Stage 3

The 1960s saw the beginning of the safety management era making line management responsible for managing risk. The safety tool kit continued to expand, including analysis, measurement, accountability and increasing involvement throughout the organization. During this stage, incident rates fell to around 8 deaths per 100,000 workers, with many leading organizations achieving much better results.

Stage 4

Although third-stage management practices worked well for most leading organizations, many company leaders continued to ignore organization-level risk management. As a result, President Nixon signed the Williams-Steiger Occupational Safety and Health Act into law on December 29, 1970. This Act authorized the federal government to set and enforce the safety and health standards still in use today.

In an attempt to comply with OSHA, many leading organizations fell back on techniques used in the first and second stages. The role of the safety practitioner shifted from manager to "compliance officer." Even this stage, fatal incident rates continued to drop to around 7 deaths per 100,000 workers.

Stage 5

Since the late 1980s and early 1990s, the safety management era continues to evolve. Modern safety management recognizes the workplace as an interaction between the work environment, the management system, and the people. Today we see the development of disciplined management systems, the reintroduction of accountability, and the recognition of behavior-based safety processes. As a result, fatal incident rates are now less than four deaths per 100,000 workers.

At what stage does your organization operate? Most firms in this country fall into one of three scenarios.

1) Doing nothing substantial to manage risk. (I.e. you are flying by the seat of your pants).

2) Using only traditional safety practices (Stages 1 and 2: inspections, safety training, etc.)

3) Managing safety as a compliance issue (focused on rule-enforcement, measurement, and standardized discipline, when necessary).

Traditional Safety Programs Yields Marginal Success

Ask yourself, has your safety program created an injury-free workplace? Or created a culture where employees and managers truly value safety?

Few organizations relying on traditional safety programs achieve marginal success from their efforts. This begs the question, why would anyone use these antiquated practices to manage safety? [Don't fix what ain't broken; would the marginal cost be worth it?]The answer is simple: because "that's how safety programs are done!" But attempts to solve a new problem with old methods rarely work, and in this case, build underperformance and create opportunities for lawsuits and catastrophic losses into their operations. Sound appealing? Yet that's the case at most companies in this country today.

Remarkably, many organizations use practices in their safety program they would never use to manage other business processes: an assortment of posters, booklets, tapes, movies, bulletin boards, displays, signs, awards, dinners, contests and games. Would you use a BINGO game to encourage productive work? One employer, for example gave his plumbers a hat, a mug, or some other trinket, for every toilet they install that doesn't leak. Another employer hung "work hard" posters beside a factory assembly line. It is hard to imagine gimmicks like these employed to manage anything important, so why do organizations continue to use them to manage safety?

The fact is, with any other key business system, employees are expected to perform because it is their job. Managers hold employees accountable for production, quality, cost, and other standards, yet use BINGO and other gimmicks to manage safety. These gimmicks make little sense in management theory and even less sense in behavioral science.

Traditional safety programs should be examined to ensure they do not undermine corporate safety efforts. A poorly designed program could easily undermine overall safety performance, erode the workplace culture, and ultimately pave the way for large lawsuits. With the erosion in workplace culture, you find faultfinding during incident investigations, incentives that discourage injury reporting, and employees disciplined for getting hurt.

The Modern Safety Management Model (MSM)

To manage safety effectively, first address the dangerous work environment, then improve the management system, and finally, address the uncertainty of human behavior. These three components form the foundation for a modern Safety Management System (SMS).

1. **Work Environment.** Considerations need to be made about environmental conditions and hazards that exist in the workplace. Assess the conditions effectively and install appropriate controls to mitigate areas of exposure.

2. **Management Systems.** Organizations must develop and implement a formal management system that outlines roles and responsibilities and uses leading indicators to ensure that all elements of the management system are implemented effectively. This means that safety must be managed like other key business functions instead of some "off shoot" or "add on". In other words, goals must be set, then the organization must plan, organize, lead and control until those goals are achieved. This is the general foundation of management.

3. **Behavioral.** People are at risk and capable of putting others at risk by their behaviors. No matter how safely a workplace is designed, and how thoroughly employees are trained, human behavior always adds an uncertainty factor. That is not to say employees hurt themselves deliberately, but they can and sometimes do expose themselves to unnecessary risk. Safety Management Systems (SMS) focuses on education, assessment, verification, and observation. A fundamental component of the modern approach is empowering employees to self-identify and mitigate workplace risks.

Behavior Based Safety (BBS)

The basic approach to modify an employee's safety performance has been branded Behavioral Based Safety or BBS for short. The BBS process involves systematically reinforcing positive behaviors, while at the same time ignoring or deploying negative reinforcement to eliminate unwanted behavior.

Before we can even attempt to discuss modifying ones behavior, it is important to understand why people take risks. We all take risks because the outcome or consequence of the risky behavior is usually positive. Take speeding in a car for example. We speed because when we do, most of the time, we get to where we were going faster. This is a very positive outcome.

Companies often reward employees for risky behavior. Paid incentive strategies such as piece rates and production bonuses is often perceived as an incentive to take risks, as long as those risks are more productive. The greater the time advantage the greater the motivation for risky behavior. What employees do not realize however, is that the short term gains of unsafe behavior do not outweigh the long-term risks. The risk-taking employee is simply gambling that the incident will not happen to them.

Since the primary psychological basis for behavior reinforcement is that behavior is influenced by its outcomes, BBS focuses on creating positive consequences to offset the inherent positive outcome of taking risks. Negative effects will decrease unwanted behavior (i.e. risk taking) while positive effects will increase wanted behavior (i.e. safe behavior).

Using BBS, the positive consequences of the safe behavior are provided by an observation process in which trained observers conduct periodic safety observations. The value of this approach goes beyond merely conducting the observation; the value comes from the feedback provided by the observer. The goal is to have the observer recognize employees who safely perform critical behaviors. Recognition is the positive outcome so desired by people. Of course, the observer also sees people *not* safely performing critical behaviors. At that time, they provide negative reinforcement to the employee to eliminate the unwanted risky behavior.

This process, when effectively implemented simply attempts to modify employees' at-work behavior. By focusing on changing employee's short-term behavior, employers are indirectly creating a workplace where safe behavior is the norm. Changing workplace norms allows a workplace culture to be constructed that will harness powerful group pressures and positively influence employees' long-term behavior.

As many managers have realized, positive reinforcement has many advantages over punishment. Creating a positive workplace culture eliminates the negative side effects of discipline and increases job satisfaction. Positive reinforcement also changes the employer/employee relationship from an overseer to a resource. It is much more powerful than negative reinforcement in both building and maintaining behavior.

Summary

Most organizations have a tendency to manage safety the way it has been managed for over a hundred years. Superior safety performance cannot be forced. This has been tried for decades with limited success. The solution to creating a true safety culture lies within the management principles of involvement and participation.

In the end, a positive safety culture will have numerous benefits in other areas as well. Morale will be higher, better management relations, and higher productivity will be the result. Any way you look at it, managing safety involves proactively identifying and controlling workplace hazards, including those hazards generated by behavior. Each system, whether traditional or behavioral, improves workplace safety, and more importantly influences the organization's safety culture.

In conclusion, Behavioral Based Safety has proven more effective at reducing accidents than traditional loss-control methods. Identifying problem behaviors is the easy part. Developing measurement tools and training staff for its deployment is where most plans fall short, especially if not supported by senior management.

One company I have seen that does a good job on creating, coaching and deploying effective BBS systems for employers is Safety Links Inc. If you would like further details on this topic, contact the owner, Trevor Reschny, CSP, CRSP at 407-760-6170 or by email at treschny@safetylinks.net. (www.SafetyLinks.net)

Let this be one of your keys for profitability.

Job Task Analysis

A job task analysis (JTA) is a quantified, objective, and measurable analysis of a job's specific and critical tasks. The frequency and force of these tasks is also documented. A comprehensive JTA includes a general job description encompassing the skills, knowledge, and abilities required.

Why is job task analysis important?

A job task analysis has numerous practical applications. Regardless of a company's size or standard industrial classification, a JTA is a fundamental component to the organization, task identification and communication enhancement within each company. A JTA is a core document shared between departments and can be agreed upon as the accepted task list per job. In addition to a written JTA, a video may be shot and subsequently edited to depict key physical demands accompanied by graphic overlays and voice narration. Human Resources, Environmental Health & Safety, Finance, and other company departments can use JTAs.

- They offer a value added, data-driven document lending specificity and a quantitative influence to a standard Job Description narrative.

- They provide a foundation for a post-offer, pre-employment Isokinetic Testing Program, Functional Capacities Evaluation or a Fitness for Duty Program.

- They help treating physicians in making objective and thoughtful modified duty and return to work decisions based on detailed information specific to a particular job and/or job site. Many physicians also report that a video JTA "brings the workplace to them," therefore, enhancing their decision-making process.

- They create supportive documentation used internally and in the claims management process.

- A document can be used to identify best practices and/or variances within a company with multiple locations and similar job duties.

- As an internal training tool, a JTA ensures new workers are fully aware of the required job tasks.

- They comprise a framework for an ergonomic assessment to assist in the identification of musculoskeletal disorders and subsequent, to implement risk management solutions.

- This tool helps employers in physical-demand planning for an aging workforce.

How is a job task analysis completed?

A JTA requires an onsite visit to the job site. Careful thought should be given to what shift or shifts should be observed. Although most job duties are the same from shift to shift, there may be duty variances between shifts. If present, those shift variances should be documented in the JTA.

While onsite, a subject matter expert interview (SME) is an integral step in the process. An SME is a worker who currently performs the duties of the job being assessed, and is well versed in the required job demands. A thorough interview adds a "first hand" perspective to the onsite observation and useful direction about what should be observed during the analysis.

Various digital measuring tools may be used during the JTA to capture the key physical demands including, but not limited to: lifting, lowering, carrying, pushing, pulling, reaching, bending, kneeling, walking, climbing, stooping, hand grip strength, pinch grips, awkward body postures, etc.

During the observation stage of the JTA, the analysts shadow one or more subject matter experts as they complete their job duties. They pay careful attention to the most strenuous and physically demanding job tasks. Routine beginning-of-shift tasks and end-of-shifts tasks that are considered routine are also analyzed to ensure start-up and clean-up duties are documented. If a particular job task is not scheduled to be completed on the day of the JTA, the subject matter expert will be asked to simulate any such activities to ensure a comprehensive JTA is completed. Since workers often understate or overstate the physical demands of their job, the observation process is perhaps the most critical element of a thorough JTA.

If a written JTA is supported by video footage, various video shots are captured of the worker completing the job's most physically demanding tasks. From the set-up process launched at the beginning of the shift to the clean-up process completed at the end of the shift, a JTA video lays out a succinct, yet convincing and educational story for the viewer.

If an employer has multiple locations with the same job in each location, it is prudent to have a JTA completed at each location, instead of using one JTA across all sites. Since there may be unique job task differences from site to site, it is important that the differences be documented and measured at each location. In the event of any claims issues or modified duty or return to work decisions made at each site, a JTA specific to the site of the injured employee assists all parties in making educated and practical decisions.

Differences in JTA's on the same job from site to site often center on equipment differences, for example, manual pallet jacks vs. electric pallet jacks or automated conveyer systems vs. mobile, manual pull out conveyers. In addition, the age of the facility may present differences in manual dock doors and dock plates vs. automated dock doors and dock plates. For these and other site-specific variances, a JTA should be completed specific to each location.

Benefits of a job task analysis?

A quantified, data-driven JTA, supported by precise scientific and digital measurements of a job's essential physical demands, provides a blueprint to organizing and explaining the basics and intricate details of a job. An employer's ability to communicate and make decisions internally is enhanced with a standard and recognized JTA. Furthermore, decisions involving the medical, legal, and insurance communities are streamlined, organized, and more effective if all parties work from the same physical demand perspective, which is driven by a JTA.

The cost savings and claims reduction costs alone provide compelling support for an employer's need to have JTA's completed on all key jobs within the company. As the key component of a post-offer; pre-employment testing program designed to screen out potential injuries to new hires, the JTA is a valuable asset to a company's risk avoidance and claims management menu.

In conclusion, a job task analysis can be a very important step in quantifying the essential job tasks and improving your operational process. It is a highly specialized area that requires expertise. A company that has done a lot of work in this area is General Management Solutions Incorporated. If you would like further details on this topic, contact the owners, Michael Leep at 804-840-2924 or by email at mleep@gmsidirect.com or Mark Willis at 757-839-8484 or by email at mwillis@gmsidirect.com. (www.gmsidirect.com)

Let this be another one of your keys for profitability.

Integrity Testing

When it comes to employment risks, a small percentage of the workforce creates most of the problems. The hard part has always been figuring out which job candidates are likely to become costly, troublesome employees.

Integrity testing is a screening tool that aims to identify prospective employees who may possess or participate in negative / counterproductive behavior. Often referred to as "self-admitting" testing, factors being measured may include any of the following:

- Theft
- Substance Abuse
- Dependability
- Honesty
- Hostility
- Impulsiveness

Identifying unsuitable candidates can save an employer problem that might otherwise arise during a term of employment.

Types of Integrity Testing

The various types of Integrity Testing fall into two categories: overt and covert.

Overt: Overt testing is very direct and often referred to as "self-reporting." Candidates taking an Overt Integrity Test clearly understand the questions being presented are about his or her behavior. The questions are not about hypothetical friends who may participate in counterproductive practices.

A sample question might ask a candidate how often they go above the posted Speed Limit while driving in the past 3 months: Never, Rarely, Sometimes, or Frequently.

Based on these types of admissions, this testing determines if candidates are "high risk" or "low risk" in counterproductive and risky behaviors.

Covert: Covert testing is closely aligned with traditional "Personality testing." These tests assess candidates by presenting them with questions that require responses about preferences or descriptions of themselves. The responses then give insight as to whether they may possess certain characteristics undesirable in the work environment. This type of testing focuses on traits such as dependability, conformity, adventurousness, kindness, etc.

Such questions ask what shapes a candidate prefers: Circles, Squares, Triangles, etc. Another asks what phrase best describes their personality: Cautious, Sensible, Adventurous, etc.

Based on the responses to these types of questions, psychologists can determine how functional a candidate will be in the workplace, whether they are dependable, and if they are likely to break company policy.

Benefits of Integrity Testing

Consistent use of Integrity Testing improves efficiency in the recruiting and selection process. It makes little sense for HR and Operations personnel to spend precious time with "high risk" job candidates who admit to counterproductive behaviors and clearly should not be hired.

Organizations using this type of testing have reported the following benefits:

• Improved workforce quality

• Reduced turnover

• Reduction in workplace violence

• Reduced absenteeism

• Fewer unemployment insurance claims

• Identification of applicants with an "entitlement mentality"

• Reduced employee theft

• Less FMLA utilization

• Major reductions in workers' compensation losses

Science behind Integrity Testing

Integrity Testing is based on the psychological theory of Cognitive Dissonance: when an individual's behavior and values are not in alignment, it causes stress. Individuals in this state of mind have either to reconcile their behavior to their values, or have to "rationalize" their actions as normal.

Such an example could be someone who smokes marijuana at work. They could either admit that this behavior is an issue, knowing it's risky and probably illegal, or they may rationalize it. "I don't know what the issue is. Other people do it around me, and it's not affecting my work, my family life, etc." Such a person has blurred the line between right and wrong.

The individual who chooses to rationalize such behaviors is suffering from Cognitive Dissonance. While this may seem an extreme example, it can present itself with attitudes towards theft, lying and even hostility.

An additional aspect of this testing is "Entitlement." Candidates with an entitlement attitude feel they are owed something or have a right to a benefit. These candidates experienced no dissonance stealing from an employer if they feel they are paid an unfair salary, or if they have issue with their employer. These employees may fake or exaggerate a workers' compensation claim, should the opportunity present itself.

Repeatedly, companies utilizing integrity testing are simply amazed at the disclosures made by candidates who suffer from these states of mind. These individuals seem to have no concern discussing their behavior, considering it normal and forgivable. In the absence of Integrity Testing, many of these high-risk applicants would get hired, potentially causing significant downstream employment costs.

Legality of Integrity Testing

Integrity Testing is a legal screening tool supported by the EEOC, as long as the test is validated and/or non-discriminatory. The ideal Integrity Test has both characteristics.

The validity of the test can be measured by how direct the questions are, and how easily they can be measured to have an impact. Is the test actually measuring what it claims to be measuring? Validated tests will be able to provide client studies showing how the exclusion of those candidates defined as being "high risk" have positively impacted turnover, absenteeism, productivity, etc. Additionally, such tests will be able to demonstrate impact on the reduction of workers' compensation loss rates.

Providers of such testing will also be able to provide you with reports pertaining to "passing rates," and the breakdowns by EEOC categories: Ethnicity, Age, and Gender. It is important to verify the test does have a disparate impact on protected classes.

Support of Integrity Testing

While Integrity Testing has been around for decades, it has recently received growing attention because it is increasingly viewed as a missing piece to the hiring process puzzle. To cite some relevant articles:

SHRM – **HR Magazine** "Your Cheating Heart" (June, 2011)

- "Research has shown that Integrity Tests have the *highest validity for predicting undesirable behaviors at work*"

Journal of Business and Psychology (April, 2011)

- "...Integrity Testing can result in *substantial savings across multiple industries*"

- "...Integrity Tests can be a useful tool to assist employers in hiring individuals who are *less inclined to engage in behaviors that are dangerous, aggressive or generally counterproductive*"

Cornell University School of Hospitality (2009)

- "...Integrity tests are a potentially *highly useful selection tool*" "*Do not create adverse impact*" and "*Produce ROI results as much as 800+%*".

Consistently, research sources find one of the primary benefits of Integrity Test screening is allowing the organization to focus its resources on rewarding performance as opposed to paying for problems.

With such support and growing awareness, Integrity Testing is becoming a more common practice and can be integrated as part of any hiring process. For more information, contact Mark Walker, Merchants Information Solutions at (570) 402-2026, or by email at mwalker@merchantsinfo.com .

Drug-Free Workplace

A. Reasons to implement a drug-free workplace program
B. State drug-free workplace programs
C. Nationwide customize drug-free workplace programs
D. Medical marijuana and recreational use clauses for a drug-free workplace policy

Reasons to Implement a Drug-Free Workplace Program

A. Some states offer workers' compensation credits to companies that comply with individual state drug-free workplace and testing guidelines. In almost every state in the nation, a workers' compensation insurance carrier will have the legal backing to deny a workers' compensation claim if an employee fails or refuses to take a post-accident drug or alcohol test. A company will also have the legal backing to deny unemployment benefits if an employee is dismissed in violation of the program. In order to qualify for workers' compensation credits, most states that offer credits require a company to conduct pre-employment drug testing on all new hires and post-accident testing on employees injured due to a work-related accident, above and beyond first aid.

B. If a company cannot or does not want to comply with the state program, they can implement a customized program to test only in desired situations (i.e. post-accident, reasonable suspicion, etc.). A company will not receive a workers' compensation credit, but will have the legal backing to deny workers' compensation claims and unemployment benefits for program violation.

C. The legal backing to test in "reasonable suspicion" cases for drugs or for alcohol is another reason to implement a Drug Free Workplace program. The definitions of what is considered to be reasonable suspicion will be outlined in the policy. If an employee meets a definition of what is considered reasonable suspicion, an employee can be tested for drugs and/or alcohol. Definitions include physical manifestations, missing money or inventory, situations related to property damage or company vehicle accidents, etc. The threat of testing if there is missing money or inventory helps reduce theft. If a suspicious case comes up and the employee refuses or fails the test, they can be fired and will forfeit unemployment benefits or have a fraudulent workers' compensation claim denied.

D. Based upon 19 years of administrating drug test results, we have come up with the following statistics. Note, statistics will be skewed due to the inability to calculate "refusals to test." This inability to include "refusals to test," which are considered to be positive, are the reason for the percentage range provided.

1. If an employer were to conduct a mandatory unannounced drug test on all employees, approximately 15-20% would fail or refuse to test.

2. About 18-22% of all post-accident tests are non-negative. This means that they are either positive, adulterated with, tampered with, or there is a prescription medication involved that showed up on the test. The legitimate prescriptions would be reported to the employer as negative once they are confirmed.

3. Approximately 20% of the positive post-accident test results are positive for alcohol at a .04 level or higher.

E. The following statistics are from the National Institute on Drug Abuse.

1. A total of about 70-75% of drug and alcohol abusers are employed.

2. Drug using employees are:

- 2.5 times more to have absences of 8 days or more,
- 2.2 times more likely to request early dismissal or time off,
- 3 times more likely to be late for work,
- 5 times more likely to file a workers' compensation claim,
- 5 times more likely to use health insurance coverage,
- 3.5 times more likely to be involved in workplace accidents,
- 10 times more likely to miss work.

How do you like those odds?

State Drug-Free Workplace Programs

Over the last 20 years, a number of states have written individual state drug free workplace laws. A number of these states will provide state mandated workers' compensation insurance credits. Each state has different requirements to qualify for a discount.

The differences are typically divided into a number of categories that may or may not apply to each state. They include:

- What must be included in the drug free workplace policy and sign off paperwork.

- The required drug testing situations (Ex: pre-employment, post-accident, suspicion,) and options (Ex: random).

- Some states require an employer to provide employee educational classes and supervisor training. They can be conducted using DVDs.

- In almost every state in the nation, an employer will have legal backing to deny workers' compensation claims if an employee fails or refuses a post-accident drug or alcohol test and deny unemployment benefits if an employee is fired in violation of the policy. In order to have the legal backing, the drug-free workplace program must be included in the policy.

States that offer workers' compensation premium credits and the credit available are listed below. All states require certain information to be included in the policy and be provided to employees. All states require drug testing in the following situations, except where noted: pre-employment, post-accident, reasonable suspicion, return to work and follow up. In all states listed below, an employer has the right to conduct random and routine fitness for duty testing, but is not required in order to receive the credit, except where noted.

States that require employee education and supervisor training will be noted.

- Alabama: 5% credit. Requires employee education and supervisor training.

- Arizona: 5% credit.

- Arkansas: 5% credit. Requires employee education and supervisor training.

- Florida: 5% credit.

- Georgia: Up to a 7.5% credit. Requires employee education and supervisor training.

- Idaho: 5% credit.

- Kentucky: 5% credit. Extremely difficult program to have approved by the State.

- Mississippi: 5% credit. Requires employee education and supervisor training.

- Ohio: Up to a 20% credit depending on the age of the program and the extent of random testing conducted. Requires employee education and supervisor training.

- South Carolina: 5% credit. Must conduct random drug testing in order to be eligible for the credit.

- Tennessee: 5% credit. Requires employee education and supervisor training.

- Virginia: 5% credit. Insurance company sets parameters for the credit.

A number of other states have laws that affect the permitted testing situations and the types of drug testing permitted or prohibited. Customized drug-free workplace policies can be written for companies that do not want to or cannot comply with the state requirements for the credit, but still want to test in certain situations and have the legal backing to deny workers' comp claims and unemployment benefits for program violation. Multiple-state policies can be written for companies operating in more than one state. The policy can be written to comply with the state guidelines of each state whether or not a credit is available.

Nationwide Customized Drug-Free Workplace Programs

Customized drug-free workplace programs are for companies that do not want to or cannot comply with state drug-free-workplace programs. State programs require pre-employment drug testing on all new hires. Typically, customized programs are for companies that do not want to, or cannot pre-employment test all new hires, but still want to test in other situations. A customized program will provide a company with the legal backing to deny workers' compensation claims if an employee refuses to test or fails a post-accident drug or alcohol test and to deny unemployment benefits if an employee violates the program and is fired. The drug testing options and implementation procedures are outlined below.

A. Drug Testing Options
1. Pre-employment and promotion into management level positions. All new hire managers and any employee who is offered a management-level promotion will be required to take a drug test.

2. Post-accident. Any employee who is injured due to a work-related accident, above and beyond first aid,

who seeks medical treatment due to the accident. A post-accident blood alcohol test can also be required for all accidents or if there is reasonable suspicion the employee was under the influence of alcohol at the time of the accident.

3. Reasonable Suspicion. The policy will outline what is considered reasonable suspicion. If an employee meets this definition of suspicion, they would be subject to a reasonable suspicion drug or alcohol test. Definitions can include, but are not limited to: physical manifestations of drug or alcohol use, confirmed reports of use, employees involved in work related accidents involving medical treatment or property damage and missing money or inventory.

4. Random. A computer generated random list that includes all employees. The company will decide on the frequency of testing and the number of employees chosen. Will be included to give the company the right to start and stop at their discretion without notice.

5. Routine Fitness for Duty. If the company deems certain employees who perform certain job duties or fall into certain job classifications are safety sensitive, the company can test those employees once a year without having to test all employees. Those employees would sign additional paperwork (Example: all managers).

6. Return to Work and Follow up. If an employee returns to work after failing a test, either as a rehire or after a suspension, they would have to pass a test prior to rehire or reinstatement and would be subject to random follow-up testing at the company discretion for 2 years as a follow up.

B. Drug Free Workplace Program Implementation Procedures

1. Decide drug-testing options to be written into the policy.

2. Decide company disciplinary action. The employee paperwork must contain a company disciplinary action on what would happen to an employee if they were ever to fail or refuse to take a required drug or alcohol test. Options would be discussed and decided upon prior to writing the policy.

3. Provide existing employees with a 30 or 60 day notice that the company is implementing a drug free workplace program. Existing employees are not tested during this period. This is their time to clean up their act prior to being subjected to any testing situations.

4. Provide existing employees with copies of the policy and have them sign paperwork acknowledging they have received the policy and understand the consequences of failing or refusing to test. This acknowledgment is kept in employee files.

5. Start drug and alcohol testing according to your policy and program.

Medical Marijuana and Recreational Use Clauses for a Drug-Free Workplace Policy

A. Medical Marijuana states-
Note: This Company is in agreement with the Federal Government that marijuana is a controlled substance and will not recognize medical marijuana as a legitimate prescription. A positive test result for marijuana will be

treated the same as any other positive test result, even if an employee has a medical marijuana prescription.

B. Medical Marijuana and recreational use states-
Note: This Company is in agreement with the Federal Government that marijuana is a controlled substance and will not recognize medical marijuana as a legitimate prescription or recreational use of marijuana as acceptable conduct of our employees. A positive test result for marijuana will be treated the same as any other positive test result, even is an employee has a medical marijuana prescription or resides in a state that has recreational use marijuana laws.

DRUG FREE WORKPLACE deployment should be a critical process in any organization. A company that has specialized in implementation and compliance is Total Compliance Network. For more information, contact Nick Mirowsky at (954) 232-5650 or by email at nickmirowsky@cs.com.
http://www.totalcompnet.com

Nurse Triage

When an on-the-job injury occurs, your employee and their supervisor are faced with multiple decisions about how to proceed. How your manager responds to these decisions can impact the total cost of your claim, as well as your employee's future health. In some instances, the decisions made at the time of injury can actually impact whether your employee returns to full-time duty or not.

These important decisions include:

- Whether or not to seek medical treatment
- What level of care that should be sought if treatment is required
    - Emergency Room
    - Clinic
- How and when a claim or incident should be reported

Your managers typically have multiple job duties and work injuries are an infrequent occurrence for them. Therefore, they may forget to follow the proper process when a work injury occurs.

A nurse triage process can assist you by helping your managers be more effective when workplace injuries occur, by acting as a third-party medical professional to help guide your managers and your employees. Triage nurses are generally available 24/7 and accessible by toll-free phone numbers. They aid injured employees in determining if medical attention is recommended for their condition and help them choose the right level of care, whether it be an emergency room or clinic. In many cases, these nurses are able to guide your employee with first aid and home care advice, which eliminates the need to set up a claim.

Additionally, nurse triage services can help you with your business processes related to work injuries. The act of taking inbound nurse triage calls from injured workers' at the time of injury allows you the ability to better guide the process and generate valuable data and reports. Benefits of nurse triage on the day of injury include:

- Channel Employees to appropriate care effectively
- Maximize PPO Network utilization
- Reduce emergency room utilization to medically appropriate numbers
- Minimize reporting lag time
- Streamlined reporting processes to save administrative time

Employees can be channeled to appropriate care effectively

In normal situations, employees injured on the job, are faced with choosing the level of care they should seek on their own or with the assistance of their manager. Generally, employees and managers have little or no medical training, so the referral is made using a "best guess" about where to seek care. In some cases, the decision is "conservative," and the employee goes to the hospital emergency room. In other cases, the decision is an "aggressive" approach, and the manager or employee makes the decision that care is not required. With their limited medical expertise, the aggressive approaches can be dangerous and the conservative approaches can be overly expensive.

Utilizing nurse triage allows a trained medical professional to get involved at the time of injury to help injured employees and their supervisors to make an informed decision on appropriate care.

PPO Network utilization can be maximized

Most established nurse triage programs maintain a directory of clinics and emergency rooms to be used as primary care for your injured employee. With that directory imbedded in the triage software, referral is a simple process. If your company has a PPO Network you wish to utilize, the triage process can be customized to reflect that network.

Emergency Room utilization can be reduced to medically appropriate numbers

Often your employees and managers will react to an injury in a "conservative" manner and choose to seek care at an emergency room. Many times, the first reaction of those with limited medical knowledge is to default to the hospital, thinking that clinics may only have very limited capabilities. Today's clinics have advanced capabilities and are able to provide excellent treatment for a wide variety of workplace injuries. Triage nurses have the training to know where to direct your injured employee and their supervisors to safely choose a referral to a clinic rather than an Emergency Room. In those cases, you can reduce your expenditures by 50% or more and be assured that your employees receive high quality medical care.

Reporting lag time can be minimized

In risk management and claim circles, it is widely accepted that earlier and more detailed reporting of workplace injuries is optimal, far better than late reporting with limited information. Earlier reporting can also make a substantial impact on the cost of claims.

Nurse triage services reduce reporting lag time for one simple reason. When someone calls in for nurse triage, they generally are calling at the moment of injury. They are calling to get help! When a manager files a claim, they are usually completing an administrative process. Whether by phone, fax or internet, claim reporting will typically be completed days and perhaps weeks after the claim occurred. Nurse triage services are accessed within minutes of the injury occurring. Thus, nurse triage reduces lag time and saves you money.

Reporting Processes can be streamlined to save administrative time

Once the nurse triage process is completed, you have at your disposal over 200 data elements that can be used to save administrative time and to improve your risk management and safety efforts. Due to the medical nature of the nurse triage process, these data elements tend to be superior in quality when compared to a normal claims reporting process which has limited clinical information.

The data gained from nurse triage can be used to populate a variety of forms for employers, saving time and money. You can use this data to populate state first reports of injury, authorization for treatment to medical providers, and even custom forms. By eliminating the need to complete forms manually, you save substantial time and allow for faster processing of valuable information. Additionally, you can use the triage data to automatically feed their RMIS and claims systems for added savings.

Nurse Triage services have grown in popularity in recent years, and have proven to have an excellent ROI. For more information, contact Company Nurse Injury Hotline.
www.companynurse.com. Paul Binsfeld (480) 222-0801. pbinsfeld@companynurse.com .

Nurse Case Management

The cost of workers' compensation claims impact the profitability of all companies through increased insurance premiums or direct dollars spent by self-insured employers. Work accidents come in all forms, from simple cuts to catastrophic injury or death. It's hard to predict with any certainty, any particular accident's eventual medical cost and outcome, because these are not always directly related to the degree of injury. Complications can arise from a variety of sources: soft tissue work injuries such as back and neck sprains or strains, aging, pre-existing medical issues, and more-involved orthopedic or neurological injuries. Left unmanaged, even relatively minor injuries can cost employers significantly. Workers' compensation carriers and/or employers may utilize case management to address these medical situations and accomplish multiple goals, including reduced costs for the claim.

Case Management is performed by qualified and certified rehabilitation nurses or, if vocational services for "Return to Work" are needed, they can be performed by certified vocational case managers. A case manager's responsibility is to deliver services required in a timely, responsive, and cost effective manner to the satisfaction of the individual and payer.

Case Management services focus on the efficient arrangement and ongoing follow-up of medically necessary service to facilitate prompt and optimal medical outcomes. The goal is to obtain objective rather than subjective information for all parties concerned. This approach can reduce the duration of disability and assure a high quality of care at an appropriate cost. Case management then becomes a process to reduce the risk and cost of Workers' compensation claims to the employer while increasing the overall efficiency of the claims process.

In a *Business Insurance* article, *"Careful Use of Nurse Case Managers Can Improve Outcomes"* author, Joanne Wojcik, writes: "Although they are an added expenses, nurse case managers can significantly reduce the duration and cost of workers' compensation claims by guiding injured employees' medical treatment and return-to-work efforts." Establish criteria up front about when and how to use nurse case managers, and continue to monitor their activities through to successful resolution of a request or file closure. It is critical that the party referring a file to case management do so in an appropriate time frame, depending on the nature of the injury and facts of the claim, so the case management professional can be appropriately utilized to assist with determining any red flags and projected obstacles to recovery and return to work early on.

Case management companies will typically bill per hour or by time and expense. Joseph Paduda, principal of Health Strategy Associates, suggests companies offer incentives to their case manager's incentives for billable hours produced; others may have required billable-hour quotas. Therefore, you will want to establish guidelines for services and rates up front with your vendor. On occasion, you may be able to negotiate a discounted or flat rate for certain referrals such as task versus full field assignments.

It is best if you decide case by case when to utilize a case manager. Establishing benchmarks and special handling instructions with your case management company, including agreed-upon rates for services, will improve your profitability and ensure you maintain control of cases assigned and costs incurred.

Rebecca Shafer, President of Amaxx Risk Solutions, has been quoted as saying "case managers also have reduced the likelihood a claimant will seek help from a lawyer" which reduces the cost of your claim. A study done by Liberty Mutual reports "nurse case managers have shaved an average of $6,100 off medical and indemnity costs for the workers' comp claims on which they were involved, producing a return on investment of 8-to-1."

The effective use of case management can:

- Reduce costs associated with injured workers' medical treatment through the coordination of care

- Enhance communication with physicians to identify treatment plans and time frames for anticipated recovery

- Offer a sounding board for the discussion of alternative medical care

- Provide medical information to the injured worker so they can better understand their care

- Support and improved communication with the injured worker to reduce attorney intervention

- Ensure effective treatment protocols and medical services are deployed

- More quickly identify and intervene on problematic areas

- Help employees feel more valued

- Minimize lost time from work and duration of the disability

- Facilitate the timely flow of medical information between all vested parties

- Oversee referrals to experienced workers' compensation providers

- Identify non-related medical conditions for treatment that are not the responsibility of the employer/carrier.

Active communication between employer, injured worker, medical provider, adjuster, and all vested parties is key to success. Nurse case management helps facilitate this. It may include the use of job analyses/descriptions or transitional duty return-to-work programs that focus on an injured workers' ability to progressively tolerate work and identify duties as they recover from their injury.

Effective communication also allows for appropriate claims decisions based on documenting the severity of a claim, establishing timeframes for anticipated outcomes, and gathering all relevant medical data, so medical providers have all available objective information at their disposal.

The oversight of referrals can help save the employer/carrier from unnecessary or high expenditures for diagnostics, medications, and services rendered. Bottom line, you want to avoid unnecessary treatment, diagnostic procedures, questionable medications, etc.

Overall, the value of case management, whether performed telephonically or face-to-face, is that it maximizes quality medical care for injured workers, while containing costs within the reasonable parameters of standardized and accepted medical practice. The return on investment to utilize case management helps employers maintain control of their workers' compensation claims and add to their profitability.

Nurse Case Management is another key that should be considered in the administration of your workers' comp program. As you can see, it takes some work to determine the viability of this service. For those companies with multiple locations in different states, I usually recommend locating a provider with a national footprint depending upon what states you operate in. One such company is Solin USA Inc.

For more information, call (407)306-6106 or email Sandra.Sweeney@solinusa.com or Gary.Livingston@solinusa.com. www.SolinUSA.com

Wellness Programs (Results-Based):

In 2008, the Department of Labor issued the Final Wellness Rules for Group Health Plans, making it possible for employers to offer incentives to encourage healthier results instead of mere participation.

The health insurance industry has been inundated with vendors offering health risk assessments, biometric screenings, health coaching and pedometers that cost a lot, but produced little measurable return on investment or clear health improvement. Employers need to understand the changing legal landscape, as well as the components of a "reasonably designed" wellness program. Then there's the question of how to introduce this radical concept without an employee revolt. The answer, according to many, is that money is the most effective motivator.

Money Motivates Engagement

But how much money does it take to motivate engagement and change behavior? Are there clear "tipping points" that maximize the investment without being viewed as unfair or overly aggressive? How do employees react to the idea of having to pay more or less than their coworkers based on their weight or their cholesterol? What about genetic issues and people with medical conditions that make goals unrealistic or even unhealthy to achieve? Some employers have achieved impressive results after implementing a well-designed wellness program.

In an industry that has struggled to achieve meaningful levels of participation in free health screenings and health risk assessment completion (http://www.towerswatson.com/research/2395), one wellness expert averaged an astounding 96% employee participation rate across its book of business in 2011.

The big difference: *Cash.*

Here's a typical design that an employer may consider:

Sample Wellness-Based Contribution Strategy:

	Non-Participant	*Pass One*	*Pass Two*	*Pass Three*	*Pass Four*
Total Premium (or COBRA rate)	*Employee pays 45%*	*Employee pays 40%*	*Employee pays 35%*	*Employee pays 30%*	*Employee Pays 25%*
Single: $400/mo	$180	$160	$140	$120	$100
Family: $900/mo	$405	$360	$315	$270	$225

Employees are in the driver's seat, determining their contribution by exhibiting healthy lifestyles.

Sample Biometric Targets to Earn Points:

Category	National Institutes of Health Goal	"Relaxed" Employer Goal	Point Value
Tobacco/Nicotine Covered Spouse Tobacco/Nicotine	Negative	Negative	1 (0 points if either fail)
Blood Pressure	≤120/80	≤130/85	1
Cholesterol	≤100 (LDL)	≤130 (LDL)	1
Obesity	BMI <25	Body Mass Index (BMI) below 30 –OR– Waist below 35-m; 32-f	1

Notice in this example the significant financial savings associated with participation alone. Then, as the outcomes-based targets are achieved, employees can earn a meaningful decrease in their cost. Employees who dispute the accuracy of their test results or report a medical issue that makes a goal unachievable for them, can typically file an appeal with their wellness administrator. The wellness administrator will work with the individual and their physician to provide a less aggressive personal goal or even a waiver of the standard.

Employees have responded well to these designs, especially when the alternative is simply to increase costs for everyone across the board. We have all had enough of that approach and the "good driver discount" was a welcome change. Today "progress goals" are the most popular adjustment employers make to their wellness plans. With progress goals, the employees earn a point because either they achieved the standard (i.e., BMI below 30) or they made meaningful progress (10% weight loss since previous screening). These goals make the program a win for virtually everyone who works at it and dramatically improves employee receptivity to "getting with the program."

Let's look at the experience of two employers that adopted results-based wellness programs.

Results: From Wellness Administrator – Bravo Wellness

Ardent Health, introduced a results-based wellness program to their 10,000 hospital employees in 2009. Consider these results:

- 94% engagement in blood draw, biometric screening, and health assessment

- Participant claims utilization decreased 3.4% while non-participant claims increased 26.8%.

- Employer's net savings: $120 per employee per year

- 16% of obese employees reduced their BMI by 2 points or more in the first year and overall, every biometric screening criterion has improved.

In the second case, Master Brand Cabinets implemented a results-based program with their 9000 manufacturing employees in 2009. They discovered equally impressive outcomes:

- 99% participation each year

- 7.6% quit smoking by year three.

- 16.4% of the obese population reduced BMI by 2 points or more by year three.

- Net of program costs, employer savings equaled $124 per employee per year, creating a great new budget that could be spent on health improvement tools and health promotion.

These results are impressive and they are typical, but they're not achieved automatically. They require a commitment from both employer and employee. It takes much more than an incentive to motivate employee behavior, cultivate a culture of health, and sustained these positive changes.

That's the great thing about results-based designs. They are self-sustaining. Those individuals who refuse to participate, or do not achieve a goal or file an appeal, pay enough of an additional contribution toward their premium that their higher contributions become the budget for the entire initiative. Best practices suggest that these dollars be invested into robust communication plans, health improvement programs and other initiatives that will help employees succeed in their quest for better health.

Bravo and many other entities from the private and public sector collaborated in 2012 to publish "*Guidance for a Reasonably Designed, Employer-Sponsored Wellness Program Using Outcomes-Based Incentives.*" http://www.acoem.org/uploadedFiles/Public_Affairs/Policies_An d_Position_Statements/JOEM%20Joint%20Consensus%20State ment.pdf , is a document that helps employers articulate the need for results-based programs and the factors most likely to inspire the kinds of outcomes reported by Ardent and MasterBrand Cabinets.

Wellness programs, implemented properly, can be an effective key for profitability. For more information, contact Jim Pshock. JimPshock@bravowell.com www.bravowell.com

Experience Modification Factor (EMF)

What is an experience modification factor?

The National Council on Compensation Insurance (NCCI) uses a complex equation with many "moving parts" to calculate your experience modification factor (EMF). Your EMF is a factor that is applied to all insurance policies and reflects how you compare to your peer group relative to the amount of workers' comp claims you have incurred over a three-year period. Your EMF can create an increase, decrease, or have no effect on your workers' comp policy premium. Sometimes the impact is dramatic.

Below is a "reader's digest" version of what an EMF is. If you'd like a more detailed explanation, go to www.NCCI.com .

Your company's EMF is affected by your losses and payrolls during the three-year period referenced above. To determine which three years of loss data go into the calculation of your EMF, look at the illustration below.

For any given experience modification year, you disregard the prior year, and look at the preceding three years.

For example, if you want to know which three years are used to calculate your 2013 experience modification, disregard 2012, and include 2011, 2010, and 2009.

Experience Mod Year

2014	2013	2012
2012	2011	2010
2011	2010	2009
2010	2009	2008

Using the same logic, your 2014 EMF will be based on 2012, 2011, and 2010. The three-year window of data used in the calculation is continually adding one year and dropping off a year.

Depending on company's payroll size, NCCI expects you to have a certain amount of claims. If your claims, when compared to your peer group, are equivalent to what NCCI expects you to have, your EMF equals 1.0. If you multiply 1.0 times your premium, it has no net effect on your premium.

If your losses exceed what NCCI expects based on your payroll size, your EMF would be greater than a 1.0, and is called a "debit mod." For example, an EMF of 1.25 means your losses are 25% higher than other companies in your peer group. This factor would be multiplied into to your workers' compensation policy, creates a 25-point increase in your premium costs.

DEBIT MOD	
PREMIUM	$200,000
X EMF	1.25
= MODIFIED PREMIUM	$250,000

If your losses are below what NCCI expects, your EMF could be less than 1.0, and it is called a "credit mod". For example, an EMF of .79, factored into your workers' Compensation premium calculation reduces the amount you pay by 21%. That's worth paying attention to.

CREDIT MOD	
PREMIUM	$200,000
X EXP MOD	.79
= MODIFIED PREMIUM	$158,000

These illustrations show the impact of the EMF on premiums. The EMF produced a $92,000 differential in premium caused by the experience modification factor. It is obviously in your best interest to do whatever you can to minimize losses, because of the effect on your EMF.

This is yet another example of how deficiencies in one part of your safety management system ripple through your organization, often multiplying costs needlessly.

Return to Work Policy

_____'s primary goal is to accommodate injured workers' by identifying or modifying jobs to meet their physical capacities and allowing them to return to work as quickly and smoothly as possible. The company is committed to individualizing return-to-work programs based around the individual's physical capabilities, and will review all task assignments regularly to ensure duties are appropriate.

We are committed to early return to work and recognize that it speeds up the recovery process and reduces the likelihood of permanent disability. _____ employees are expected to show the same commitment to the program by following the Return to Work Policy and all guidelines of the Return to Work Program. The Return to Work Program requires a team approach, so employees are expected to cooperate with the management team, supervisors, and medical staff, should they ever become injured and unable to perform their full job duties.

Prior to working on any _____ job site, each employee is expected to have read the entire Return to Work Policy, which includes the following sections:

- Purpose
- Scope
- Applicability
- Responsibilities
- Procedure
- Refusal to Participate
- Family Medical Leave

If you have any uncertainty or questions regarding the content of these policies, you are required to consult your supervisor. This should be done prior to signing and agreeing to the _____ Return to Work Policy.

I am aware of and have read _____'s Return to Work Policy, and I understand the requirements and expectations of me as an employee. Should I become injured or ill and unable to carry out my regular duties, whether it happens inside or outside the workplace, I fully recognize _____'s expectations of me during my recovery. I also know that _____ reserves the right to pay less than my full-duty rate during transitional work if it is justified.

I understand that if I choose not to participate in the Return to Work Program or follow this policy's guidelines, I may become ineligible for state workers' compensation benefits and, in some cases, my refusal may be grounds for termination.

_____

Employee Signature:

_____

Date:

Drug-free Workplace Policy

The goal of _____'s Drug-Free Workplace policy is to balance our respect for individuals with the need to maintain a safe, productive, and Drug-Free environment. The intent of this policy is to offer a helping hand to those who need it, while sending a clear message that illegal drug use and alcohol abuse are incompatible with working at _____.

All employees are expected to understand and actively participate in this program. _____ encourages its employees to take a proactive approach in identifying potential problems or violations by promptly reporting them to their supervisor. It is the employee's responsibility to be aware of the following violations:

1. It is a violation of our policy for any employees to possess, sell, trade, or offer for sale illegal drugs or otherwise engage in the use of illegal drugs or alcohol on the job.

2. It is a violation of our policy for anyone to report to work under the influence of illegal drugs or alcohol - that is, with illegal drugs or alcohol in his/her body.

3. It is a violation of our policy for anyone to use prescription drugs illegally. It is not a violation of our policy for an employee to use legally prescribed medications, but the employee should notify his/her supervisor if the prescribed medication will affect the employee's ability to perform his/her job.

4. Violations of this policy are subject to disciplinary action ranging from a letter of reprimand, to suspension from work without pay, up to and including dismissal.

If you have any uncertainty regarding the content of this policy, you are required to consult your supervisor. This should be done prior to signing and agreeing to the
_____ Drug-Free Workplace Policy.

I have read and understand _____'s
Drug-Free Workplace Policy, and its requirements and expectations of me as an employee.

_____

Employee Signature:

_____

Date:

Employee Safety Handbook
Employee Acknowledgement Form

_____ is firmly committed to your safety. We will do everything possible to prevent workplace accidents and are committed to providing a safe working environment for you and all employees.

We value you not only as an employee, but also as a human being critical to the success of your family, the local community, and
_____.

You are encouraged to report any unsafe work practices or safety hazards encountered on the job. All accidents/incidents (no matter how slight) are to be immediately reported to the supervisor on duty.

A key factor in implementing this policy will be the strict compliance to all applicable federal, state, local, and
_____ policies and procedures. Failure to comply with these policies and procedures may result in disciplinary actions.

Respecting this, _____ will make every reasonable effort to provide a safe and healthful workplace that is free from any recognized or known potential hazards. Additionally, _____ subscribes to these principles:

1. All accidents are preventable through implementation of effective Safety and Health Control policies and programs.

2. Safety and Health controls are a major part of our work every day.

3. Accident prevention is good business. It minimizes human suffering, promotes better working conditions for everyone, holds _____ in higher regard with customers, and increases productivity. This is why _____ will comply with all safety and health regulations that apply to the course and scope of operations.

4. Management is responsible for providing the safest possible workplace for Employees. Consequently, management of _____ is committed to allocating and providing all of the resources needed to promote and effectively implement this safety policy.

5. Employees are responsible for following safe work practices and company rules, and for preventing accidents and injuries. Management will establish lines of communication to solicit and receive comments, information, suggestions, and assistance from employees where safety and health are concerned.

6. Management and supervisors of _____ will set an exemplary example with good attitudes and strong commitment to safety and health in the workplace. To this end, management must monitor the company's safety and health performance, working environment, and conditions to ensure that program objectives are achieved.

7. Our safety program applies to all employees and persons affected or associated in any way by the scope of this business. Everyone's goals must be to constantly improve safety awareness and to prevent accidents and injuries.

Everyone at _____ must be involved and committed to safety. This must be a team effort. Together, we can prevent accidents and injuries and keep each other safe and healthy in the work that provides our livelihood.

By signing this document, I confirm the receipt of _____'s employee safety handbook. I have read and understood all policies, programs, and actions as described, and agree to comply with these set policies.

_____

Signature

_____

Date

Glossary of Terms

Best Practices - is a method or technique that has consistently shown results superior to those achieved with other means, and that is used as a benchmark. In addition, a "best" practice can evolve to become better as improvements are discovered. Best practice is considered by some the process of developing and following a standard way of doing things that multiple organizations can use.

Claims management systems (CMS) - is a software application for the administration, documentation, tracking, and the reporting of insurance claims.

Experience modification factor - Experience modification is a factor assigned to your company by the National Council on Compensation Insurance (NCCI) based on your prior loss history.

NCCI determines what the "average" loss experience is for a particular workers comp class code and then they compare your history against that average. If your workers comp loss history has been better than the average then your experience mod will be a factor less than 1.00. If your loss history has been worse than the average you will be assigned a factor above 1.00. Once the factor has been established your workers comp premium is then multiplied by that factor for that year.

A company's eligibility for an experience modification is based on the amount of workers comp premium. In order to qualify for an experience modification in Florida you must have an average annual workers comp premium of $5,000 or more for at least 24 months during the "experience period". Employers that have not been in business for at least 5 years will be assigned an experience modification of 1.00 also known as a "unity mod".

Your experience modification is calculated on a yearly basis using three years of loss history. The three years of loss history usually exclude the most recent prior two years and uses the three years behind that.

Incurred losses - Losses are incurred when they happen. The total of all such losses (whether paid or not) make up this figure as it appears on the company operating statements. This figure is one used frequently for various periods as well as in the annual statement. It would take much work to keep track of losses both by date of occurrence and payment. The figure is arrived at by subtracting from the period's paid losses those which were on the books unpaid at the beginning of the period and adding those which are on the books unpaid at the end of the current period.

Indirect loss costs - After you quantify the costs of insurance and direct loss costs to your organization, including deductibles or retentions, you should also consider the indirect loss costs. If you think of a claim or injury as an iceberg, you will find that the majority of the accident costs lie below the surface. These indirect costs are much more difficult to quantify and therefore, they may go unnoticed by your organization. Experts contend that the indirect costs of accidents and injuries can exceed the direct loss costs by as much as seven times.

Here are a few indirect loss costs.

- Administrative costs to administer the claim and the resultant damages.

- Higher workers' compensation experience rating, which increase premiums.

- Lost productivity due to retraining.

- The cost to hire temporary workers to meet production goals or staffing requirements.

- An inability to meet pre-injury production benchmarks.

- Replacement or downtime of damaged equipment or tools.

Integrity testing - Many employers are now using honesty or integrity testing to determine an employee's suitability for particular jobs and attempt to minimize theft, embezzlement, or filing of claims against the employer. These may include written psychological tests designed to predict employees who are more likely to engage in conduct against the employer's interest.

Learning management systems (LMS) - is a software application for the administration, documentation, tracking, reporting and delivery of education courses or training programs.

Loss ratio - The difference between the ratios of premiums paid to an insurance company and the claims settled by the company. Loss ratio is the total losses paid by an insurance company in the form of claims. The losses are added to adjustment expenses and then divided by total earned premiums. So if a company pays $80 in claims for every $150 in collected premiums, then the company has a loss ratio of 53%.

Net profit margin - A ratio of profitability calculated as net income divided by revenues, or net profits divided by sales. It measures how much out of every dollar of sales a company actually keeps in earnings. A higher profit margin indicates a more profitable company that has better control over its costs compared to its competitors. Profit margin is displayed as a percentage; a 20% profit margin, for example, means the company has a net income of $0.20 for each dollar of sales.

RiskScore® - is a quantifiable benchmark that companies use to determine their standing in relation to the deployment of best practices in the administration of operational policies and procedures that reduce business risk. What can be learned from an *RiskScore®* are the strengths and weaknesses of those policies and procedures that reduce business risk.

Total Cost of Risk - The sum of all quantified costs and expenses associated with the risk management function of an organization. Total Cost of Risk = Insurance costs + retained losses + risk management departmental costs + outside service fees + indirect costs.

Workers' compensation coverage – The insurance that protects employees under state laws, and provides medical care, death, disability and rehabilitation benefits for workers who are injured or killed while on the job. The insurer agrees to pay all compensation and benefits related to the insured employer's state's workers' compensation laws. Workers' compensation coverage premiums are based on the employer's payroll and the type of duties its employees perform.

Workers' compensation system - denotes the holistic approach to the administration of a workers' compensation program and its coverage. Utilizing a system enables you to reduce your Total Cost of Risk by deploying operational policies and procedures that reduce business risk.

Bibliography

Note: During the course of writing this book, I interviewed top specialist from the insurance, safety, HR, and legal communities. Their contributions made it possible to focus on the top issues confronting companies coast to coast, and on ways to prevent potentially catastrophic losses by taking a proactive stance to workplace health and safety.

Adler, Ron. Laurdan and Associates. HR Consultant Date of Interview: 1/11/2013   2305 Glenmore Terrace, Rockville, MD 20850

Binsfeld, Paul. Owner, Company Nurse, LLC. Date of Interview: 12/10/2012

Bob Norton. C Level Enterprises http://tiny.cc/xva9rw

Ekern, Rob. Consultative Brokerage: A Value Strategy USA, 2007

Ford, Frances. Co-Owner, Re-Employability, Inc. Date of Interview: 2/6/2013

Hammond, Keith. Attorney at Law, Labor Law Specialist. Date of Interview: 1/29/2013

Kidd, James. Attorney at Law, Workers' Compensation Specialist. Date of Interview: 1/9/2013

Leep, Michael. Co-owner, General Management Solutions, Inc. Date of Interview: 12/3/2012

Miguel Lianos, 7/12/2011. <u>2011 Already Costliest Year for Natural Disasters</u> (Online) email: miguelllanos@feedback.msnbc.com

Mirowsky, Nick. Total Compliance Network. Date of Interview: 12/6/2012

Powell-Yoder, Eleanor. President, MCIM Insurance Company. Date of Interview: 12/9/2012

Pshock, Jim. President, Bravo Wellness. Date of Interview: 1/28/2013

Reschny, Trevor. President, Safety Links, Inc. Date of Interview: 12/12/2012

Sweeney, Sandra. President, SOLIN USA. Date of Interview: 1/9/2013

The National Underwriter Company

Walker, Mark. Merchants Information Systems. Date of Interview: 1/8/2013

Willis, Mark. Co-owner, General Management Solutions, Inc. Date of Interview: 12/3/2012

Larry Bossity and Ram Charan, Execution: The Discipline of Getting Things Done.

Affiliate Links

If you're reading the hard-copy edition of this book, for easy access, just cut/paste URL address (below) into your internet browser.

4 Keys to Competitiveness in the New Economy
http://keysforprofitability.com/?p=68

Want to Know Where You Could be Losing Profits?
http://keysforprofitability.com/?p=76

If You Don't Do This, It Can Cost You Big Money
http://keysforprofitability.com/?p=78

Are You Well Positioned for What's Ahead?
http://keysforprofitability.com/?p=80

Reduce the Cost of Your Claims by 70%...See How & Why
http://keysforprofitability.com/?p=82

Experience Mod Factors expected to increase
http://richarddalrymple.com/experience-mod-factors-expected-to-increase/

Six Strategies to Reduce Work Comp medical Costs

http://www.prlog.org/11763055-6-strategies-to-reduce-workers-compensation-medical-costs.html

Recession, Recovery, & Workers Compensation Claims
http://richarddalrymple.com/recession-recovery-and-workers-compensation-claims/

Do You Know Your RiskScore - Key to Profitability
http://richarddalrymple.com/do-you-know-your-risk-score%e2%84%a2-%e2%80%93-key-to-profitability/

Hiring Practices – Key to Profitability
http://richarddalrymple.com/hiring-practices-%e2%80%93-key-to-profitability/

Return to Work – Key to Profitability
http://richarddalrymple.com/return-to-work-%e2%80%93-key-to-profitability/

Claims Management Systems – Key to Profitability
http://richarddalrymple.com/claims-management-systems-%e2%80%93-key-to-profitability/

Learning Management Systems – Key to Profitability
http://richarddalrymple.com/learning-management-systems-key-to-profitability/

NCCI Changes for 2013
http://richarddalrymple.com/ncci-changes-primary-excess-split-point-for-2013/

Four Dangerous Trends Facing your Business
http://www.prlog.org/11782142-4-dangerous-trends-facing-your-business.html

About the Author

Rick Dalrymple is an owner and Senior Vice President of IOA Risk Services, a division of Insurance Office of America, a risk management and insurance brokerage firm whose clients serve a vast array of industries such as manufacturing, hospitality, healthcare, retail, wholesale and professional sports teams.

With over 25 offices coast-to-coast, his company has taught CEOs in over 300 industries how to lower the number and cost of insurance claims. He consults nationally with many CEOs, C-Suite and administrative executives on how to lower their "*Total Cost of Risk*". His 40,000+ hours of experience consulting are visible in the results his clients receive.

His clients experience double-digit reductions in employee turnover, claim costs and frequency after implementing their "PX4" process in as little as 6 to 12 months.

Rick has served as a keynote speaker for numerous associations and is transforming businesses all over the country with his message on how to avoid, minimize, or eliminate business risk that impact profitability.

His presentation is rich in content, focused on providing a new way to understand business risk and delivers new tools to compete more effectively.

Contact information:

IOA Risk Services LLC, a division of Insurance Office of America

Rick Dalrymple, CPIA, CMIP
1855 West State Rd. 434
Longwood, FL 32750

Office: 407-998-4108 Cell: 321-578-7559

Email: Rick.Dalrymple@IOAUSA.com

Corporate Web site: www.IOAUSA.com

Personal Web site: www.RichardDalrymple.com

LinkedIn: http://www.linkedin.com/in/rickdalrymple

For public workshops, contact Rick at
Rick.Dalrymple@ioausa.com

Do you need a speaker for an Association meeting or a National Convention? Call our office today.

A few of the Associations and industry groups served:

- *International Window Cleaners Association*

- *Scaffold & Access Industry Association*

- *Florida Association of Electrical Contractors*

- *Refrigeration & A/C Contractors*

- *Society for Human Resource Management*

- *Wall & Ceiling Contractors*

- *Air Conditioning Contractors Association*

- *Association of Homes & Services*

- *Florida Restaurant & Lodging Association*

- *Marine Contractors Association*

- *Association of Diesel Specialist Manufacturing*

- *Health Care*